O's

Little Book of
Love & Friendship

Other Titles in O's Little Books Series

O's Little Book of Happiness

O's Little Guide to Finding Your True Purpose

O's

Little Book of Love & Friendship

—❖—

The Editors of *O, The Oprah Magazine*

MACMILLAN

First published 2016 by Flatiron Books, New York

First published in the UK 2016 by Macmillan
an imprint of Pan Macmillan
20 New Wharf Road, London N1 9RR
Associated companies throughout the world
www.panmacmillan.com

ISBN 978-1-5098-0803-8

1 3 5 7 9 8 6 4 2

A CIP catalogue record for this book is available from the British Library.

Printed and bound by CPI Group (UK) Ltd, Croydon, CR0 4YY

Visit **www.panmacmillan.com** to read more about all our books
and to buy them. You will also find features, author interviews and
news of any author events, and you can sign up for e-newsletters
so that you're always first to hear about our new releases.

And I know for sure that in the final analysis of our lives—
when the to-do lists are no more, when the
frenzy is finished, when our e-mail inboxes
are empty—the only thing that will have any
lasting value is whether we've loved others
and whether they've loved us.

—Oprah Winfrey

Contents

Just You and Me

In love, one and one are one.

—JEAN-PAUL SARTRE

The Four-Alarm Wedding

Andrea King Collier

I was freaking out. I went to bed the night before, freaking out. What was I doing? What was he doing? We were twenty-six, and we were getting married. It was such a bad idea—clearly we were too young. Everybody knows the true best age for a first marriage is forty-five. I remember getting a brown paper bag and breathing into it that morning. I was sure he wouldn't show up. *I* thought about not showing up. It was awful and wonderful. It felt like going to the guillotine in a really fabulous dress.

Years later I have come to realize that there are two things that happen. Two people get married. And two people have a wedding. These things don't really have a lot to do with each other. I wasn't worried about being a wife that day; I was worried about being a bride. I should have given more thought to the whole wife thing, but I was twenty-six and it was all about the right wedding music. What if our relatives got drunk? Of course somebody was going to get drunk—it wouldn't be a wedding if they didn't. Getting married wasn't going to throw me over the edge, but being a bride was surely going to finish me off.

One of my mother's dear friends had left an emergency wedding-day Valium for me. She told my mother that she would know when to give it to me. My mother produced it right about the time I got back in bed with the covers over my head and the balled-up paper bag in my hand. "Here, take this," she said.

The next thing I remember is being at the country club where we were going to get married, wearing shorts and a T-shirt, rollers in my hair, and, miraculously, a full face of makeup. I thought it was a good idea to go out and greet the guests—before the wedding. I was so calm and charming and gracious. Fifteen minutes before the wedding was supposed to start, I still had on shorts and big green rollers in my hair. And Darnay, the groom, was not there. He and his best man were watching a fight on television. Twenty-six is too young to get married. I am sure that people who were watching this spectacle were shaking their heads trying to figure out if we would return their gifts in a week when we got divorced. The oddsmakers would have had a field day.

But somehow, the girl with the big green rollers and the guy who forgot that he had to be somewhere survived the wedding and built a marriage—which, a quarter century later, is still a work in progress. It almost seems astounding that we've made it this far. In spite of ourselves we were able to raise our kids, create and re-create careers, argue over who should be doing the laundry, and learn how to trust each other more than we trust anybody else. We have had great joy in our years together, and we have shared a lot of sadness and loss.

When I was twenty-six years old, holding my head between my knees, breathing into a paper bag, I didn't know I was about to go on a wild adventure. I surely didn't know I would grow into a really good best friend to someone who would learn how to be a best friend, too. When we celebrated our anniversary this year, there were no big parties. The bride and groom—the husband and wife—wore sweatpants and dirty gym shoes. We ordered a pizza. We drank water because we've read that soda increases heart disease in old people. And we had to eat before six because, these days, the bride gets acid reflux. This time around there was a paper bag, too—with cheap reading glasses, and ibuprofen for the groom's creaky back and the bride's popping knees. And just like the first time, everything went off without a hitch.

I Love You, You're Perfect, Now Scram

Cathleen Medwick

The taxi is just pulling out of the driveway. He is on his way to Indonesia, a five-day business trip. Gone! I don't know what to do first. Take a walk outside with just a noisy bunch of tree frogs for company? Cue up some highly objectionable music (that would be the soundtrack to *Carousel* or *Show Boat*) and raise the volume to deafening? Or sing! I'm great on the choruses, even the solos—I've been listening to this music since I was ten.

Let me catch my breath for a moment. My husband has left the building, and I'm exultant; it's the way you'd feel if you landed alone on the moon and everything was cool and silvery and you knew you could go home to Earth again—just not quite yet. Because I'm crazy about Jeff, my husband of thirty-two years. All that time, we've had coffee together practically every morning. We've bought dinged and battered antiques that nobody else would look at twice. We've lived congenially, for the most part, in a one-bedroom apartment, a rambling prewar Classic Six, and two drafty, centuries-old exurban farmhouses with sodden basements (doesn't *every* house have water seeping through its limestone foundation?). I've handed him a glass of vodka as he obsessed about his dozens of orchids and his acres of flax, and I've shrieked at him as he uprooted the tender shoots of our fifty-year-old peonies with the rake of his tractor. I've seen his eyes close in rapture as he played his guitar; watched him gaze with boundless admiration at our sweet, manic quasi-Labrador, and even at me. I've seen him accumulate a world-class collection of ties—enough to outfit a small company—and a pile of laundry so steep it finally collapses into the bathroom doorway, where he nimbly climbs over it, scattering clothing like rose petals in his wake. I've watched him sleep propped up on his elbow, head resting in his hand and blankets merrily twisted around his legs, as the eternal light from the blaring television flicks hectic patterns onto his face. I've listened to him snore so resoundingly that our neighbor's peacocks honk in solidarity. And I've tip-toed out of the bedroom, slippers in hand, to slide beneath the covers of our daughter's bed (she's long been out of the house), where the velvety night envelops me and I can hear the humming of my own reclusive mind.

In truth I have always been a loner. I love tiny, singular spaces where a body can sit quietly and contemplate. I was never happier than when I lived in my quirky basement apartment in a Manhattan brownstone, and Jeff, a stranger to me, moved into the parlor-floor apartment right above it. We began to meet for coffee, and at night after he got home from his corporate job at a textile firm and I finished reading for my graduate courses in Renaissance poetry, I'd clamber upstairs and sip wine with him. I might stay over—or I might go downstairs to sleep alone. It wasn't exactly Jean-Paul Sartre and Simone de Beauvoir maintaining separate apartments and perfectly calibrated minds. I have no idea what Jeff and I talked about in those early days, but it was probably nothing more scintillating than how I could prep for my orals without falling asleep and whether or not he should paint contrasting trim around his ceiling. It didn't matter. What mattered was that we never stopped talking.

Then we moved in together, into his apartment. I had to get rid of my spindly Victorian furniture; it looked ridiculous with his chunky brown sofa and pragmatic oak table and chairs. The shag rug was a bone of contention; luckily, it didn't survive a sheepdog with digestive issues. Crammed in a claustrophobic space, we began to battle, one of us invariably slamming the door and retreating into the narrow bedroom. We built a sleeping loft to escape to. Still, we not only survived the merger but married. We tried to become a "we," traveling for our honeymoon to the Paris I loved (and he hated), always seeing friends together, dragging each other to movies that bored one of us to death. His eyes glazed over when I tried to fascinate him with *Middlemarch*. I rubbed my temples while he replayed a Hendrix album into the wee hours or puzzled over some intricate business deal. We survived corporate dinners and foreign films, poetry readings and rock concerts.

My role models were artists, his were entrepreneurs. We tugged persistently at each other's psyches and prayed for continental shifts.

As the years passed, though, the tugging became less strenuous, more habitual. We perfected the fine art of needling. Our children, Lucy and Peter, grew up exasperated but also oddly liberated by our differences, which at the very least gave them options; one eventually became an editor, the other a musician, and both are avid readers who seriously love rock music. Gradually, it dawned on us that we, too, had grown up. Or we had aged out of social insecurity. We no longer had to prove anything to others or, for that matter, to ourselves. We knew we could trust each other. We could say goodbye when we went to work in the morning, maybe stay in town to meet a friend (someone the other could live happily never seeing), and reconvene at home later to compare notes. It was never boring. It's still not. Yet I have friends who tell me they do everything with their husbands. They push a cart together at the supermarket. (Jeff: "I'd rather be dead. Just let me do the shopping.") They never travel separately. If I ask a childhood pal (now married) out to dinner in hopes of some intimate conversation, she invariably answers, "We'd love to!" Calling a friend in California, I learn that "we" are dazzled by the new exhibition at the Getty; we're vegan now; we saw that movie and we were not amused. I relate more easily to my ex-roommate Ginger, who rolls her eyes in mock gratitude when her stay-at-home husband sallies out alone; to my grad-school friend Jane, who has a heady and deeply satisfying relationship with a man who lives in another state, but worries about what will happen to their blissful independence if the two of them ever move in together. I can see her point. Sartre and de Beauvoir lived apart until their deaths, after which some enterprising soul decided to plant them under a single headstone. They've got to be turning in their grave.

I walk out the door with a suitcase, on my way to speak at a weekend writers' conference in Texas, as Jeff, guitar pick in hand, laptop softly whirring in the next room, gives me the warm, sweet glance I fell for decades ago, and a parting kiss. He tells me to have a wonderful time as he gently and firmly closes the door. I know he's about to celebrate—three days in which the television never goes off, the dog sprawls on the bed, the lights stay on till three A.M. No one greets him at daybreak with a list of ancient grievances and a furrowed brow. No one smashes his concentration as he's putting the finishing touches on a complex lecture or presentation. No one gloomily reports to him about diseases he doesn't have and dangers he's too sanguine to fear. He's in paradise, and he's got it all to himself. When I finally return, exhilarated by the readings and the company of other writers, he will be delighted to see me. He will have already opened a bottle of wine, and the porch chairs will be ready and waiting. We will have so much to say.

The One

Allison Glock

This is a love story. Like every other, and like no other. This is a story about how one day I believed certain things about myself and the next day I knew, the way you know a good nectarine, that I had been wrong.

About all of it.

This is what real love does, of course. Transforms. Enlightens. Boils off the fat. Reveals the sinew underneath. I had read about such things in poems. Sung along with the heartbreak songs. But I had not felt that sort of love myself. The kind that shakes you up inside like a Boggle board, jangling all your letters into wholly new words, some you've never seen before but recognize instantly nonetheless.

It started with a misunderstanding. A misunderstanding that in the end wasn't a misunderstanding at all.

I first saw my love online. He had written something about music in a column I often read. The column comes with a photo of the author. And it was the photo, more than the words, that captivated me. It was nothing extraordinary. Just a head shot. Him, looking sleepy-eyed and stoned (which, as it turns out, he was) in a brown shirt and narrow tie. He was sitting down, slumped and easy, and it was obvious even from the pixilated screen of my decade-old computer that this man was unlike any other I'd known. I found myself staring, leaning in as though he were an insect on the sidewalk. There was something about him: intelligence, warmth, confidence, but also something else. Something I had no name for.

That night I went to see *Slumdog Millionaire* with my mother. I told her about the photo. "He looks like Dev Patel," I said. He did look like Dev Patel, but I was so consumed, everything I saw looked like him. The popcorn guy. The theater curtains. The shadows on my windshield as I drove home from the movie. Late that night I gazed at the photo again. And I decided I would send this man an e-mail. From all angles, this seemed crazy and pathetic to me. What kind of fool writes an unsolicited note to a complete stranger? It wasn't as if I had an agenda. I didn't. I expected nothing. But not writing seemed somehow impossible. I was drawn, impelled.

I wrote two lines: introduced myself, said I'd seen the article. And pressed *send*.

He wrote back the next day. This in itself was a small miracle. As a successful novelist, my intended receives a lot of uninvited e-mail. He even has an assistant to weed through the letters, answering most with a cursory *Thanks for your interest and support* note. But this e-mail he read himself. And though it said nothing particularly charming or saucy or brilliant, he felt he needed to respond.

And so we began. The old-fashioned way, with letters chaste enough to show your grandmother. We did not Google-stalk. Nor did we write about our similar careers or engage in eager, romantic self-promotion. Instead, we stayed in the present, wrote about who we were, who we wanted to be. It was the opposite of flirtation. We talked about our mistakes. Our families. Our needs. Neither one of us was selling anything. It was unlike any courtship, any conversation I had ever had. The intimacy was so immediate, the compatibility so palpable, we didn't notice until it was too late that we'd grown hooked on transparency, on the dizzying, terrifying high of finally allowing ourselves to be seen.

It was amid all this that my love disclosed something that should have mattered. Something the whole of my history would have insisted mattered, and yet, did not. Not really. He told me, in his typically open, candid style, that he had not been born male.

"This will never work," says my friend Ralph the day after I find out. We are having lunch. Ralph is a chef, bald and brawny, the kind of guy who can get away with wearing a red leather coat. He shakes his head, sloppily scooping Vietnamese noodles into his mouth. Ralph has known me since I was twelve years old. He has seen the men I have cycled through over the years: the brutish painter, the boxing steelworker, countless football jocks and rednecks and martial artists, culminating in a civilized eight-year marriage to a onetime Australian rugby player that produced two daughters and one of the more amicable divorces on record.

"You aren't a lesbian," he says in between slurps of his noodles.

"He isn't a woman," I answer.

Ralph rolls his eyes. "At any rate, you like manly men. Testosterone is your Kryptonite."

He isn't wrong. The last man I was involved with was six foot four, another ex-boxer, who grew up on the South Side of Chicago and so reeked of conventional masculinity that he was cast as cops and toughs in major motion pictures.

"Plus," Ralph adds, looking pointedly down at his crotch, "there's this little issue."

"Your napkin?" I say, narrowing my eyes.

"More like what's under the napkin," he says drily.

And there it was. The first incidence of what I would soon learn to be the defining question about my relationship with a trans man: What the hell, if anything, is under the napkin?

When you date a man who was not born male, people have questions. Most of these questions are about sexual relations. Some are astonishingly bold, as when a good friend requested I draw her a picture of what my boyfriend's privates looked like.

Then there was my mother, who, upon hearing that my online beau and I were officially an item, blurted out, "Does it even work?"

Trans men are used to these queries, invasive and inappropriate as they may be. This is still a man's world—men earn more, control more, are valued more—and what makes a man is nothing less than the key to the cultural castle. But if the only true definition of manliness is "one who possesses a working penis," that poses an interesting dilemma for the guy who's suffered, say, an unfortunate lamb shearing accident. And what about men with negligible penises? Are they only ten percent male? How about men who require pills to make their penises elevate? Are they men only when medicated?

"But, Ali," my mother says, lowering her voice to a whisper, "you're not gay."

This rapidly becoming-familiar conversation is happening at an old-fashioned tearoom in Florida. There are doilies on the tables, women with oxygen tanks wheezing nearby. I myself struggle to breathe, trying to explain how gender and sexuality are not the same thing, how someone can know himself to be a boy even if he was not born with the boy kit. How nothing is clear-cut, if you are honest about it: girls play football, boys like to sew, everyone cries. How society has made the rules, issued the uniforms and the lists of approved activities, but where it counts—in your heart, in your head—the truth is always far blurrier.

My mother takes a long sip of iced tea.

"You mean he's like RuPaul?"

"RuPaul is gay, Mom. He's a drag queen, not transgender."

"Isn't your boy gay?"

I sigh.

"No. He is a heterosexual man. Like Dad."

"He is not like your father," she gasps, looking from side to side. "Your father is normal."

Okay. Perhaps my boy is not a "normal" boy. This is true. But normal has always felt like a lie to me, a too-tight sweater we force ourselves to wear. Normal has never been too kind to women, children, people of color, people mired in poverty, anyone different in any way. Normal is good for no one, really. It is a lie we all decide to believe. After even the most cursory look, no one is actually normal; it is a plastic bag we wrap around our own heads.

Besides, I tried normal.

I was fourteen the first time I had sex. His name was Kenny. He was an older boy I'd met that night at Skate Road 13, a roller-skating rink near my house.

"You have long-ass legs," he'd said, shaking back his

oily, shoulder-length hair as we sat hip to hip during the hokey-pokey.

I didn't like Kenny. But he had a car and keys to an apartment, and I was a mixed-up girl whose birth father had flown the coop—"He fooled us all, Ali," my grandmother would wail—and whose new daddy seemed constantly at war with her mother, daily accusations hurled like bottles, shattering everything that was once beautiful in their lives.

"Men are full of shit," my mom would spit, scrubbing the sink with bleach until her knuckles cracked red.

Watching her sob in the laundry room, I ached for something that felt like power. So I slept with Kenny, a boy I didn't like. Then, months later, his friend Billy, whom I liked even less. It was easy.

Easy to say yes when I meant no. Easy to confuse pleasing with power. Easy to bury myself alive in the passing desire of another. Easy to pretend I had no wants of my own, beyond making that boy happy for that moment. It was easy, and like most easy things with intense but quickly dissipating payoffs, it became a habit.

Nobody blinked. Because it was normal.

Raised in the South, I was taught that women existed

to provide a service: to reflect the successes of men. So I did what many women do: I became a walking mirror, choosing men who would see only what I showed them. Men pleased to be looked after. Men who would not try to look after me. For twenty-eight years I stayed hidden, running the show, getting it done, avoiding intimacy like rotten meat.

Then I met my Dev Patel, my "not normal" man, and the mirror disintegrated into glorious, glittering dust, the old, hardened me along with it. He broke me the way I was broken the first time a child reached to hold my hand to cross the street. I was unlocked, redefined, filled up in an instant with feelings as hard to bury as elephants.

"Tell me everything; you know I love a tranny!"

I am drinking margaritas with my old friend Liz. She wants to know what is under the napkin. More, she wants to know where I see this thing going.

"How is your mother handling it?" she asks, eyes wide.

"Surprisingly well," I say. She then asks if there has been any blowback.

"We're not exactly getting sent congratulatory bouquets," I say. Then I tell her someone in my family had described my new love as "it" and said if he came any-where near him, he'd "kick its ass."

"Jesus," Liz says, licking salt off her glass.

I shrug, tell her how I've never been happier, how I don't recognize myself, how everything seems possible, blessed, easy.

"You have a boy with a girl brain," she says, dreamily. "It is the best of both worlds."

Not exactly, I think, remembering how my man mani-cally flips the channel on the remote control, cruising for any show with a pit bull or a medical trauma or a cop. Or how his eyes glaze over when I ask if I look fat. Or how often he thinks about sex.

"His brain isn't exactly feminine," I try to explain. "He's pretty much a dude through and through. He's even color-blind."

"No kidding?" Liz says.

"And he won't let me drive."

"Sounds like a guy to me."

The next morning at home, I watch my man brush his teeth. He vigorously works his toothbrush for at least five minutes, till the foam covers his mouth clown-style. He leans into the sink, one arm crooked on the edge. He is short, five feet five to my five feet ten, and slight. His curly brown hair spikes up in the front like Astro Boy's. He spits enthusiastically then turns and grins, the white of the toothpaste still coating him nose to chin.

"Do I have something on my face?" he asks, feigning confusion.

He kisses me, leaving a slick of foam on my cheek, then shuffles off to get dressed, walking even in those wee A.M. hours like a man rich with confidence.

My eyes track him. I think, *God, he is handsome.* I think, *How could anyone look at him and not see who he is meant to be?* I think, *If I were any more in love, I'd be unbearable company.*

He comes back into the bathroom, asks what is on my mind.

"Nothing," I mutter.

"Liar," he says, catching my gaze.

I do not tell him the truth—that the best future I can imagine would be to watch him brush his teeth every day for the rest of my life.

Several years back, my love was on the subway in New York City when some young thugs put a knife to his throat.

"You think you're a man?" they hissed. "You trying to be like us?"

My love said nothing, made himself very still and quiet. The thugs nudged him, knocked the side of his head, poked his chest, then grew bored and exited the train.

When he tells me this story, I try not to worry.

"This was before I had my mustache," he jokes, brushing his hand across the black fuzz emerging on his upper lip, one of the effects of testosterone therapy.

I don't laugh. I am drowning inside. Terrified that this man, this gentle, generous, brilliant man, could be in danger simply because of who he is. *This is America*, I think. *The land of reinvention. Why would anyone even care?*

But some people do care. Certain men, especially. Men who resent anyone crashing the boys' club without an invitation, daring to take power where none was given. Which, if you think about it, is the genesis of every human rights movement in history.

"I don't want any harm to come to you," I whisper in my love's ear while he sleeps.

I watch his face, his chest moving up and down, and I wonder, *How did this big love happen?* A love so bright I can only sneak glimpses of it, anything more igniting me like tissue paper. And then I remember the letters, the first date, the tumbling of wall after wall, both of us putting down our shields, taking long looks, allowing what we felt to trump what we'd been told to think.

And then there was the moment, early on, when he was washing dishes and instinctively cupped his hand over the sharp edge of my kitchen drawer to protect my daughter's forehead from a scratch. That moment alone told me all I needed to know about who this man was, and what he could be for my children. Without even knowing, he passed me hope, clear and simple as a plate.

"I like him," my nine-year-old said that night when I tucked her into bed. "He's not like other boys."

A few hours later I am cradled tight in my love's arms, something that, in other relationships, always made me feel confined, uncomfortable. He is looping his fingers through my hair, tucking it behind my ear. We lie like that for hours, breathing slow, saying nothing.

"I'm going to take care of you," he says, finally. "Whether you need me to or not."

"I don't need you to," I protest. "I've never needed any-one to . . ."

"Even so," he chides, pinching my cheek firmly.

My love and I are getting married.

"Real married," he always clarifies.

His driver's license lists him as male, as does other essential paperwork, edits that were simpler than qualifying for a Sam's Club card. According to the government, he is officially a man.

"Now if your mom could just get her head around the Jewish thing," he jokes.

I do not love my fiancé because he is trans or in spite of his being trans. I love him because of who he is, the same reason he loves me. And the rest dissolves, as it did in the beginning, when he was just a boy smirking from a photograph.

There are rare challenging days. "Ladies" days. Days when the well-meaning waitress or dishwasher salesman will be confused by my man's slender frame and mistakenly ask how we "ladies" are doing, prompting him to shrivel in front of me like a dropped leaf. Usually, he says nothing. Unless it is date night, and we are having drinks and appetizers and we have dressed up in our Saturday finest—he in a jacket and tie—and the third or fourth "ladies" tips him into a concise but always mortifying rebuttal.

"Excuse me, but I'm a guy."

An apology usually follows. Which makes it even more awkward, because he doesn't want anyone to feel bad or sorry, he just wants to be seen the way he sees himself.

I think about this sometimes. How I would feel if I were called "sir" while I was on a date, wearing a dress and heels and cherry lipstick. How abnegating it would be to have the world look at you and decide, no matter how many signals you give, that you are something you are not.

There is a misbegotten notion that trans men and women are about playing dress-up and fooling people. But to be trans is to feel the truth so acutely you can't fake it. It is to be so consumed with the truth of who you are that you are willing to risk everything to inhabit it. To refuse to be what other people have decided you are—this is an act of courage few individuals dare try. I know I didn't.

It is late fall, and we are walking through the woods with the girls, searching for birch bark and tossing sticks to the dogs.

"This is the first time I've ever stopped wondering where I'm supposed to be," my fiancé says as we climb a slight hill, all of us hand in hand. I start to cry. So much sweetness, such simple tenderness.

We talk about the holidays, the kids' soccer matches; we talk about the wedding, a year from now, my dress, my hair, whether or not he should wear lifts, like Andre Agassi did when he wed Brooke Shields.

"I need every inch I can get," he says, a wink in his voice.

We banter and tease, and I giggle, flip my hair. I am drunk with optimism, skipping through leaves, looking for unicorns in the clouds. And I realize then that this man has done something I never thought possible. Something revolutionary.

He has made a girl out of me.

The Love List

Alice Bingham Gorman

Our first real disagreement erupted at the kitchen table on a Saturday morning in late May. Aubrey and I hardly knew each other at the time. We had spent a total of three weekends together since we met in early March—the first on a blissful fishing trip in the Ozarks, the other two trading visits between his home on the Eastern Shore of Maryland and mine in Memphis. He was a recent widower; I, a divorcée and a widow. He was retired. I was the owner of a contemporary art gallery in Memphis and a partner in a gallery on Fifty-seventh Street in New York City. We'd been introduced by his cousin from Baltimore, a lifelong friend of mine. The attraction was instantaneous, so much so that we spent those six days together in pure enjoyment of our late-in-life pleasures and commonalities, believing that each of us had found perfection in the other. But without warning, during our second cup of coffee after breakfast, we began having a stupid argument.

"You're really a stubborn broad," Aubrey said in response to my refusal to spend the remainder of the morning with him.

"What do you mean?" I asked, shocked by his insulting bluntness. "I told you I had to go to the gallery on Saturday morning. I have an appointment with an artist. You knew that."

"You told me you *might* have an appointment on Saturday morning, but if I flew down to Memphis for the weekend, you'd change it."

"I did *not* say that," I said, stiffening my spine and feeling my heart begin to race. "Obviously you didn't listen to me, and now you're calling me a liar."

"You see," he said with a grin. He had a wide smile that generally dispelled the seriousness of any discussion, but he continued to make his point. "You're a stubborn broad. It's your way or the highway."

"Well, what about you?" I felt sickened as waves of ancient marital arguments surged up through layers of memory. I'd thought Aubrey would be different. "Aren't you the one being stubborn?"

Aubrey sat back in his chair. "Maybe I'm not the right man for you," he said, half making a statement, half asking a question.

"Maybe you're not!" I crossed my arms, feeling defiant, but in the next second I regretted the whole ridiculous discussion. What were we talking about? I thought I had met the man of my dreams, and we were about to throw the whole thing out the window over an absurd argument.

Closing my eyes, I suddenly saw a mental picture of "the list." It had been in the back of my closet for five years. What would Aubrey think of the list?

"I have an idea," I said. I left the kitchen, and several minutes later I came back holding a small sheaf of papers. "Read this, and you decide if you are the right man for me." I turned on my heel and marched down the hallway to my room, as if following stage directions.

Five years before meeting Aubrey, I was in despair. Still dealing with the residue of a divorce after twenty years of marriage, then the tragic death of my second husband—a shocking result of his manic depression—plus several love affairs and a broken engagement, I was emotionally exhausted. When I wasn't actively juggling the demands of the art business in two cities, I found myself sinking into bouts of tears and despondency, trying to dispel the fear that I would never have a true and lasting love in my life. Then one day a close friend called to suggest that I make an appointment with a clairvoyant who was visiting Memphis. "She's fabulous," my friend said, and proceeded to tell me all the insights and factual information the psychic had revealed to her. Dismissing the skeptic in my head, I thought: *Why not? What do I have to lose?*

After speaking with the woman—a cheery voice on the telephone—I drove to an ordinary, small brick house on an ordinary street. The woman who opened the door had a friendly face and a mop of curly reddish hair. "Hi there," she said, as if we knew each other. "I'm Charlene. I'm glad you've come." She showed me into the living room, a sparse space with a rocking chair next to a standing lamp and a straight-back chair across from it. The blinds were drawn, making the room feel like twilight in the middle of the day. "Sit here, my dear," she instructed, pointing to the straight-back chair. She sat down in the rocking chair and lit a candle on a small table under the lamp.

"Now, tell me," she said. "What is it you have come to ask?"

Before I could speak, my throat filled with tears. I felt as if I were a small child desperately trying to stay above water in a pool. I started to gasp.

"Do not worry, my dear," Charlene said in a mossy-soft voice. "You are safe here."

Her voice was a sort of balm. I swallowed several times as if flushing away years of unspoken fears.

"Now, tell me," she said again, "tell me why you're here."

"I want to know if—" I began, but I couldn't finish the sentence. Finally, I blurted out: "I want to know if I am supposed to have a true and lasting love in my life. It's okay if I'm not. It's really okay. I have so much in my life. My family. My friends. My artists. My galleries. I just want to know. I want to stop worrying about it—thinking about it all the time."

"Let us see," she said, and she closed her eyes.

We both sat in stillness for a matter of minutes, then

she cocked her head toward the ceiling, and her voice became high-pitched and singsong. "Well, my dear, the real question is: What is it that you truly *want* for your life?"

I began to feel the tears forming again. "I want to share my life," I said. "I've always wanted to share my life. But it seems that I am destined to be with the wrong person. It always ends in disaster. I don't know. Maybe I am not supposed to share my life."

"My dear." Charlene's lilting voice filled the room. "The spirits say that you should have *exactly* what you want. They say that of course you should share your life if that is what you want."

I took a deep breath. I could feel the tension leaving my body. "Really?"

"Yes, of course," she said. And as if she were repeating instructions from the spirits, she told me, "Here is what you must do. You must go home and write down one hundred qualities you would like this person with whom you will share your life to have."

I felt almost giddy. "A hundred? Wouldn't I be lucky if I got ten?"

"Oh no, my dear," she said. "You must describe the person down to the color of the socks!"

I wanted to laugh. The color of the socks?

"You will make your list, and then you will put the list away for safekeeping. What you are doing is making clear for yourself exactly the person who will be right for you, and then you will be directing the request into the universe to send that person to you. Do you understand?"

I nodded. But I didn't understand at all. The idea that somewhere in the universe was a person just right for me—someone who would respond to all the things that were important to me and with whom I could share my life—seemed impossible. Yet in spite of the painful experiences of the past, I had always lived my life as if all things were possible. Why wouldn't I try making the list?

At home I climbed into my four-poster bed with a yellow legal pad. I was amazed by how easy it was to write the list. I began with the definitive idea that he must be "at peace with himself." And I went on to cover everything from good family relationships to intelligence and a sense of humor, to sex, religion, money, music, books, gardening, sailing, dancing, fishing, and on and on—down to dark gray socks.

Satisfied that I had done my part, I put the list in the back of my closet.

After about fifteen minutes of waiting for Aubrey's answer, he walked into my room with the list in his hand and tears in his soft blue eyes. We looked at each other for several seconds before he spoke.

"I missed two," he said, holding up the list. Then, smiling, he added, "There are many things on this list that are true about me that you could not possibly have known."

I wanted to laugh out loud. Instead I jumped up and threw my arms around him. I felt jubilant. However certain I might have been that he missed many more than two, I knew the point was that *he thought he missed only two*. I had given my list to the universe and the universe had sent me Aubrey.

Addendum: Aubrey and I were married in February of the following year, the beginning of a gloriously happy and trusting time in my life. Of the two qualities on the list he thought he missed—"loves to dance" and "loves to sail"—neither was important. His interests in gardening and architecture, previously unknown to me, led us to build a house and garden in Maine that surpassed either of our dreams. Some of the more intangible qualities on the list provided even greater surprises. We shared eleven wonderful years before he died of lung cancer, many more joyful years than I had ever imagined possible. What happened was beyond all reason. I can only marvel at the mysterious and beneficent universe that brought us together.

The Tricky Bits

Intimacy is a difficult art.

—VIRGINIA WOOLF

Lover's Leap

Martha Beck

—✢—

Psychologists tell us we're born afraid of just two things. The first is loud noises. Do you recall the second? Most people guess "abandonment" or "starvation," but neonatal dread is simpler than that: It is the fear of falling. Today we all have a much richer array of terrors, but I'll bet falling is still on your list. Why give up the prudent concern that brought your whole genetic line into the world clutching anything its tiny fists could grab? Fear of falling is your birthright!

Perhaps that's why most of us, at least some of the time (and some of us most of the time), are frightened by another deeply primal experience: intimacy. Allowing yourself to become emotionally close is the psychological equivalent of skidding off a cliff, hence the expression "falling in love." This gauzy phrase usually describes a sexual connection. But love has infinite variations that can swallow the floor from under your feet at any moment. You're securely installed in a relationship, marching through life, keeping your nasal hairs decently trimmed. Then, boom! You hear a song and know that the composer has seen into your soul. Or you wake up, bleary with jet lag, in a city you've never seen before, and feel you've come home. Or the wretched little mess of a kitten you just saved from drowning begins to purr in your arms. Suddenly—too late—you realize your heart has opened like a trapdoor, and you're tumbling into a deep, sweet abyss, thinking, *God, this is wonderful! God, this is terrible!*

The next time this happens, here's a nice, dry, scientific fact to dig your toes into: The sensation you're feeling is probably associated with decreased activity in the brain region that senses our bodies' location in the physical world. When this zone goes quiet, the boundary between "self" and "not self" disappears. It isn't just that we feel close to the object of our affection; it's that perceiving ourselves as separate isn't an option. Some being that was other now matters to us as much as we matter to ourselves. Yet we have no control over either the love or the beloved.

The horror! The horror!

As a culture, we are drawn to stories about people, from Othello and Huckleberry Finn to the lusty physicians on *Grey's Anatomy*, who trip into versions of intimacy (passion, friendship, parental protectiveness) they can neither escape nor manage. These stories teach us why we both fear and long for intimacy—and why our ways of dealing with it are usually misguided. Two of these ways are especially common, and especially unhelpful.

Bad Idea #1: Guard Your Heart

There's an old folktale about a giant who removes his own heart, locks it in a series of metal boxes, and buries the whole conglomeration. Thereafter, his enemies can stab or shoot him, but never fatally. Of course, he also loses the benefits of having a heart, such as happiness. The giant sits around like Mrs. Lincoln grimly trying to enjoy the play, until he's so miserable he digs up his heart and stabs it himself.

This grisly parable reminds us that refusing to love is emotional suicide. Yet many of us fight like giants to guard ourselves from intimacy, boxing up our hearts in steel-hard false beliefs. "I'm unlovable" is one such lockbox. "Everyone wants to exploit me" is another. Then there's "I shouldn't feel that" and "That would be against the rules," etc. Whatever your own heart-coffins may be, notice that they're ruining your happiness, not preserving it. As the poet Mary Oliver puts it,

> *Listen, are you breathing just a little, and calling*
> *it a life?*
> *. . .*
> *For how long will you continue to listen to those*
> *dark shouters,*
> *caution and prudence?*
> *Fall in! Fall in!*

If you've buried your heart to keep it from hurting, *you're* hurting. You're also in dire danger of embracing Bad Idea #2.

Bad Idea #2: Control Your Beloved

"If you don't love me, I'll kill myself. If you stop loving me, I'll kill you." Some people believe such statements are expressions of true intimacy. Actually, they're attempts at domination that destroy real connection faster than you can say "restraining order." Though few of us are this radically controlling, many of us use other forms of manipulation and coercion. We can say, "Sure, whatever makes you happy," in a tone that turns this innocuous phrase into a vicious blow. To the extent that we try to make anyone do, feel, or think anything—whether our weapon is sarcasm or a machete—we trade intimacy for microterrorism. But if neither control nor avoidance works, what does?

Good Idea #1: Be Willing

In *The Ultimate Hitchhiker's Guide to the Galaxy*, Douglas Adams reveals the secret of flying. Just launch yourself toward the ground, and miss.

> *All it requires is simply the ability to throw
> yourself forward with all your weight, and the*

willingness not to mind that it's going to hurt . . . if
you fail to miss the ground.
Most people fail to miss the ground, and if they are
really trying properly, the likelihood is that they
will fail to miss it fairly hard.

This is the best advice I know for coping with fear of intimacy. Avoidance and control can't keep our hearts from falling, or cushion the landing. So why not try throwing yourself forward, being willing not to mind that it's going to hurt? Please note: "Being willing not to mind" isn't the same as genuinely not minding. You'll mind the risks of intimacy—count on it. Be willing anyway.

How? Simply allow your feelings—all of them—into full consciousness. Articulate your emotions. Write about them in a journal, tell them to a friend, confess them to your priest, therapist, cab driver. Feel the full extent of your love, your thirst, your passion, without holding back or grasping at anything or anyone (especially not the object of your affection). Here's how:

Good Idea #2: Go *Woohoo*

Author Melody Beattie took up skydiving and was scared senseless. Another diver told her, "When you get to the door and jump, say *woohoo*. You can't have a bad time if you do."

This phrase works as well when you're falling emotionally as when you're falling physically. When fear hits, when you want to grasp or hide, shout *woohoo* instead. While there is never—not ever—a sure foundation beneath our feet, the willingness to celebrate what we really feel can turn falling into flying. You don't need an airplane to practice *woohoo* skills. For instance: I'm writing these words at two fifteen in the morning because writing, like other intimate pursuits, often occurs at night. As I type each word, I come to care about how it will be read—about you, there, reading it. And caring is scaring. It makes me want to stop right now, or spend years composing something flawlessly literate. Unfortunately, my deadline was yesterday, and Shakespeare I'm not, so . . . *woohoo*!

Now it's two twenty A.M.. My writing partner, a fat, aged beagle named Cookie, snores contentedly at my feet. I'm revisited by a worry that was born the day I fell in love with his puppy self: the dread of the moment when that snuffly breathing will stop. This is my cue to throw myself forward and drop deeper into my affection for this ridiculous dog. Tomorrow I will let Cookie teach me to roll in the grass, to howl in ecstasy at the sight of good food. Of any food, actually. *Woohoo!*

Now it's two thirty A.M.. Upstairs, my son, Adam, is dreaming dreams I'll never quite understand, because his brain is different from mine. Shortly before his birth, I learned that he had Down syndrome, which put mothering him well above skydiving in my *Book of Fears*. I yelled a lot during Adam's birth. Eighteen years later, I'm still yelling *woohoo*. And so far, the only consequence of that particular plunge is love.

Which brings me to my final point.

What I really panic about nowadays isn't falling; it's landing. But even that concern is fading because I've realized there are only two possible landings for someone who embraces intimacy, and both are beautiful.

The first possibility is that your beloved will love you back. Then you won't land; you'll just fall deeper into intimacy, together. This is how bald eagles prepare to mate—

by locking talons and free-falling like rocks—which is deeply insane and makes me proud to call the eagle my country's national bird.

The other possibility is that you'll throw yourself forward, yell *woohoo!*, and smash into rejection. Will it hurt? Indescribably. But if you continue refusing to bury your broken heart or force someone to "fix" it—if you just experience the crash landing in all its gory glory, you'll create a miracle.

A Jewish friend told me this story: A man asks his rabbi, "Why does God write the law on our hearts? Why not *in* our hearts? It's the inside of my heart that needs God." The rabbi answers, "God never forces anything into a human heart. He writes the word on our hearts so that when our hearts break, God falls in." Whatever you hold sacred, you'll find that an unguarded broken heart is the ideal instrument for absorbing it.

If you fall into intimacy without resistance, despite your alarm, either you will fall into love, which is exquisite, or love will fall into you, which is more exquisite still. Do it enough, and you may just lose your fear of falling. You'll get better at missing the ground, at keeping a crushed heart open so that love can find all the broken pieces. And the next time you feel that vertiginous sensation of the floor disappearing, even as your reflexes tell you to duck and grab, you'll hear an even deeper instinct saying, "Fall in! Fall in!"

My Learning Curve

Walter Kirn

First comes love, then comes knowledge. And that's the whole problem: You feel before you think. You drink from the glass before you know what's in it, and you only begin to taste it once it's down.

What I've learned about love is that I never learn.

I should have learned the first time, but I didn't. I was seventeen and she was twenty. She was a dancer, or wanted to be a dancer, and I fell for her when I first saw her perform.

The song was something stupid by Tom Petty, but her outfit was as tight and bright as the shine on an apple. We spoke after the show, but what we spoke about I don't remember; all I remember is wanting to wedge my hand between her spandex and her skin. By the time I got the chance to do that, it was clear we had not a single interest in common except for our interest in each other. Which wasn't enough, as it turned out.

Then I did the same thing again, with variations, and made the same old mistake in a new way. This time it was a picture that caught my eye and dragged my brain along after it—a book-jacket photo I came across while browsing in an airport bookshop. I liked her looks but I also liked the fact that we shared a vocation: writing novels. No more inarticulate dancers for me. No more thick silences in cars and restaurants. I wrote a letter to the woman, and when, against all odds, she wrote me back, I flew thousands of miles to New York to take her out. Our first date was a mere formality, though, because I was already in love with her, and particularly with the long talks about art and life and so on that I'd never been able to have with the cute dancer but that I knew I'd have with the lovely writer, and did have.

The last of these talks took place in couples therapy when the woman and I decided to part ways. I asked the therapist what I'd done wrong. "You acted without deliberation," she said. Her answer baffled me. If I'd deliberated, I felt, I might never have acted at all. Still, I took her words to heart, and for several years I deliberated thoroughly every time a woman piqued my interest. The result was . . . nothing. I did nothing. The moment I felt an infatuation start, I argued myself out of it by thinking ahead to the ways it might end. But then someone grew infatuated with me, a possibility I hadn't counted on, and I, undeliberately, decided to let her.

Fooled again. It never stops. First comes love, then comes knowledge. The problem is that it's new knowledge each time, and it doesn't accumulate into lasting wisdom. It seems to, but it doesn't. Indeed, in my experience, applying the lessons from a past romance to a present romance is the surest way to ruin it. I know this because I've tried. And always will.

Sixteen Again

Abigail Thomas

It was fun while it lasted, and it lasted three hours and forty-five minutes, from six forty-five until ten thirty. That's when the restaurant closed. It wasn't a blind date because I'd seen him around, first at Yum Yum Noodle Bar, where he looked gentle and gallant, and next at an art opening, where he looked angry. I was struck by his angular face, and I asked a friend if she knew who he was. She nodded, saying she thought he was an artist. "I love the way he looks," I said. A week later he turned up in the audience of a concert my friend gave, and afterward she told him she knew a woman who'd like to meet him, but the woman was shy. "Tell her that if she doesn't call, I won't eat for a week," he said, which charmed the hell out of us. He (let's call him Luther) gave my friend his number and e-mail so I could get in touch. The telephone was more than I could handle, so I e-mailed. We made plans to meet the following Monday.

The best way to prepare for an evening out when you're pushing seventy is to put the blue eyeliner on before you make coffee in the morning. Eyeliner always looks best after being napped in, blinked on, and showered with, and over the span of a day achieves the smudgy look so prized by Egyptians. The same is true for blush. Put a lot of it on early, and as the day passes it may begin to look natural. I recently found out that if your face is as lined as mine, it is better to use cream than powder. I had always thought it was the other way around. "Put it on the apples of your cheeks," said the pretty young woman who had also asked as tactfully as she could if I spent a lot of time in the sun.

"Every chance I get," I told her.

By six forty-five both blush and eyeliner looked perfect. I wore a black skirt and a red velvet shirt and my best flowered Betsey Johnson tights, since my ankles are now my best feature. I showed up on time. Three young women were ahead of me in line, whispering, then one turned around and shyly declared that she loved my books. I thanked her, we blushed, and they were shown to their table. *What a lovely way to begin an evening,* I thought. *Oh, I wish Luther had seen it,* I thought.

I had prepared myself to see Luther's face fall when we met, but he betrayed no disappointment or surprise. Hello and hello, a pleasant shaking of hands, we took a seat at the bar. He was handsome. His shoulders were like great big folded angel wings. He was tall. His face was bony and also very deeply lined, and he looked as if he made things. We ordered drinks. I had a Manhattan; he had a ginger ale. *When did you stop drinking,* I wondered, because he didn't look like a man who'd been ordering ginger ale all his life.

Was I hungry? Oh yes. We moved to a table by the window overlooking the icy creek I can never remember the name of.

I think I loved him from the moment he looked at the menu, read *petit rack of lamb,* and asked the waitress how big the portion was. "That's just what they call the way they cut the chops," she explained, "nothing to do with size." He had the lamb and I forget what I had. (I never forget what I have.) We talked about making things; we talked about how he began a sculpture, "with a gesture," he said,

Sixteen Again | 59

swooping his arm in the air. We talked about what he did after the gesture part was over, and what he did was a lot like what I do with writing—figure out what it's all about by heading off in different directions—and it was all very exciting. He talked about the boring suburb where he grew up, and how in his early twenties he had become a wilderness leader. Then when he was proficient at everything—rivers, mountains, rock climbing—"there was nothing left," he said, "but to take acid and go into the woods." Acid scares me to death, and so do the woods. I asked if he'd ever had a bad trip. He shook his head. "The trick is to get out of the house in time," he said.

"When did you stop drinking?" I asked.

"Eight years ago," he said.

We looked out the window at the creek, the shifting patterns of dark water and thin pale ice, and the flat rocks on the bank. "I have already recorded the shape and color of those stones," he said. This reminded me of Matt Damon telling Franka Potente, "I can tell you the license plate numbers of all six cars outside," but I didn't say so.

Somebody bought us a round of drinks. The waitress wouldn't tell us who; they wanted to be anonymous. I thought maybe it was the nice young woman who had spoken to me earlier. "No tip unless you tell us," Luther said, but she kept her secret. I kept wanting to lean across the table and kiss him. "Hold still," I wanted to say. I hadn't felt like that in twenty years. We were still talking when we realized the restaurant was closing. We split the bill, got up to leave. He introduced me to two friends still at the bar, both of whom were named John. Then we left. He peered into the back of my car and mentioned something about the dog food there. "I'd love to do this again," I said, and he said something I didn't hear because I was opening the car door.

I got home and called my friend. "I had the best time," I said. "I just love him."

I never saw him again. I e-mailed him after a day or two, saying I hoped he'd had as good a time as I had and asking him a quick question about something he'd said. "Who was it who said, 'Man wants but little here below, but wants that little longer'? Was it Oliver someone?" Of course I knew the answer.

His reply was brief. "Yes, Goldsmith, but not *but*, it's *nor*." Not another word.

Oh my God, I thought, *you're a* dick*!*

But being seventy has its advantages. I did not spend

any time wondering what I'd done wrong, or what I could or should have done differently, whether I was too old or too fat or asked too many questions. I am who I am, and it has taken me a long time to get here. But part of me was sad, because I liked him, and we did have a good time. The date was like an island you stumble on with a stranger, and you spend a few pleasant hours together there, but you can never find the island again. I ached a little.

And then, oh God, I suddenly remembered waiting for a glimpse of my first serious crush, Tony Wallace, as he drove up or down the hill outside our house. It was 1956, I think. I swear I could hear his car coming forty miles away, and I'd rush to the window hoping for a glimpse of his elbow sticking out the driver's side if he was driving up the hill, or a girl in the passenger seat if he was driving down. Either way I was filled with love and longing, an ache that was almost pain. Tony was tall and gentle and beautiful with sad, sad eyes. He was a few years older than I was. He had asked me out a few times, and it was he who taught me how to French kiss on that hill overlooking the Hudson, the smell of wisteria everywhere, but finally I was just too young. *Oh Tony,* is all I'm thinking now.

Where are you?

She's a Big Cheese, He's a Little Annoyed

Andrew Corsello

My wife is radiant. It comes naturally to her. Yes, she's very beautiful, and that beauty is the first thing people notice and discuss about her. But hers isn't the radiance of a model or a starlet; it's a radiance that emits warmth—*love*—as well as light. What Justice Stewart said of obscenity can be said of Dana's radiance: Words fail, but you know it when you see it. *Yup, there it is.*

Dana is in the radiance business. Literally—she's an Episcopal priest. But while she's been radiating through-out the three years of our courtship and the eleven of our marriage, something's changed in the last nine months. Thanks to this ever-crescendoing glow, I am typing these words while looking out at San Francisco Bay from the top floor of a big and beautiful house I could never afford were I actually required to pay for it. It ought to go without saying that I type with glee. Yes, it ought to. And yet, despite the Jiminy Cricket perched on my shoulder yelling, *Stop the whining!* until he's red in the face, there is a degree to which the bounty of my wife's radiance has left me feeling a little, well, irradiated.

As well as robbed of one of my favorite punch lines. "And what do you do, Andrew?" I've been asked at countless cocktail parties over the years, and if I'd not yet reached that evening's joke quotient by introducing Dana as "my first wife," I'd say, "Oh, I'm a preacher's wife." I was quick with that joke because I could afford to be; because as everybody around us presumably understood, I was the dynamic force in the life we were building together, the sun around which all else revolved. I suppose this arose in part from our relative incomes; my annual earnings always doubled and sometimes tripled hers. But mostly it arose from my being a magazine writer—from years of training and straining to be a voice, *the* voice, in the stories I wrote, and in my own domain.

Perhaps I should mention that I have a big fat ego. Huge. Hungry. Hairy in all the wrong places. Want to see it? Be glad to show it to you. That's who I am. It's how I do. Yet in terms of the algebra of our marriage, the ego has always . . . worked. Since I can do what I do for a living from anywhere, it's Dana's job prospects that determine our geography. And the ego has always blinded me to the fact that my wife has dragged me all over the continental U.S. The ego is what has allowed me to look in the mirror each morning and think, "There he is, the Big Enchilada," even as I've trailed my woman like a lapdog.

But then suddenly, last summer, everything changed. After a rigorous, nearly yearlong winnowing process, St. Luke's Episcopal Church in San Francisco named Dana its first female rector. In August we moved from Richmond, where for eight years she had been the associate rector of a large urban parish. Christian vow of poverty? Please. The new job comes with a rectory, which is another way of saying that we live in a giant house adjacent to Pacific Heights—for free; we don't even pay our own freaking utility bills. The wonders my wife's radiance has wrought! Extraordinary private schools (Episcopal, of course) that we would otherwise have had little chance of getting our sons into. The list goes on.

You know where this is going, right? Yup: I did nothing

to procure this wonderful life—I couldn't have done it if I tried—and I DON'T LIKE IT. Something within me, something disoriented and not a little bit petty, keeps protesting that this is not the deal I signed up for, that this is not my beautiful house; yes, even that this is not my beautiful wife!

And I know what you're thinking: Just an unreconstructed chauvinist pig who can't handle his wife wearing the pants. But I believe something else, more fundamental, less about power and more about self-understanding, is going on.

Dana now runs one of the signature churches in one of America's signature cities. She's a persona, a position, the face of that church. And the face of our marriage, our family, our life. In San Francisco, it's crazy but I swear to God it's true, I am no longer the magazine writer Andrew Corsello. I am no longer even Andrew Corsello, period. I am the spouse of the rector of St. Luke's Church. She took my name when we married, and now she's *taken* it; in this town, *Corsello* means her, and it's only by her beneficence that I'm allowed to partake of it.

I expected people to perceive my wife differently in San Francisco than they did in Virginia. She's running the show now, and that commands a qualitatively different kind of regard. I also expected that, as in Virginia, our social life would be largely, even entirely, a function of our church life, especially with us living in the church rectory and all. The part of our deal I didn't see coming was the qualitatively different regard I now "command" in our life. I am no longer seen directly by others; I am refracted through my wife. And the unspoken question I feel pressed upon me everywhere I go in my new city is the same one politicians' wives must contend with: Does she stand by her man? In other words, do I attend church every Sunday? Do I choose an up-front eager-beaver pew or one toward the back? Do I kneel or stand during the creeds and prayers? Do I believe as she believes? Back in Virginia, Dana wasn't the boss of our church, much less of me, and I was regarded as an outlier, a dude—which lined up nicely with my own notion of myself. Now I am reflective of her and responsible to her—rather than for her—in a way that unmans me. And surprises me: When I vowed "for better or for worse," I considered the various ways, however theoretical, that "worse" might rear its head. But who ever considers, much less braces himself for, the possibility of his betrothed becoming radically "better"? And *bigger*?

I am proud of Dana. How could I not be? I knew she

was going to kick butt once she was in charge. She is a called person, and I did expect miracles. So it's an elation to see her doing not only better, but far better, than I thought anyone could in her position. The Sunday Show she puts on each week rocks. But as with all committed clergymen and clergywomen, eighty percent of her job isn't public. It's the one-on-one work, the pastoral visits and confessions, her whole immersion in the deepest joys and griefs—the addictions, the betrayals, the diseases and deaths—of her parishioners' lives. To be married to a truly gifted woman of the cloth is to be married to a woman whose thirty or forty closest friends are perpetually and overlappingly on the brink of the abyss. The demand for Dana's psychic energy and love is many times greater than it was before she replaced me as the Big Enchilada. Yet she somehow has it in her to give commensurate with what is needed. So I have spent the last nine months watching in amazement as her radiance has amplified.

A small problem, then, is that her spouse happens to be a person to whom attention must be paid. Undividedly. Rapturously. Ceaselessly.

For a time I acted out in little childish ways, tried to reject this New Deal of hers and mine, and my assigned role in it. I would approach her in the receiving line after the Sunday ten A.M. service, behold the alb, the stole, the resplendent finery of her station, look into her beautiful, kissable face and then try to make her flinch by whispering, "Girl, you put the *ho* in *holy!*" Or the *lay* in *Revelation*. Then, one day, out of nowhere and out of everywhere, I turned to her as we were reading in bed and said, "Baby, let's make a deal."

I told her I was having trouble recognizing myself. I told her that as much as I liked this new life she had created for us and for our boys, I felt inescapably *part of*—a member of—a flock. I needed to reclaim my self. "Like a wolf pissing out its territory," I told her.

She said, "Of course, darling. Anything. I want you to be happy."

"Okay, then," I said. "Here's the deal. I've found a small cabin in the middle of nowhere outside Buena Vista, Colorado"—my home state. "I need to buy it. I need to make it mine, ours . . . whatever."

"Do it," she said.

"And you need to agree that I can go there by myself

at least four times a year," I added. "This is part of the deal."

"Do it," she said again.

So I did.

So far, I've spent three separate weeks there. It's a beautiful place, a dream. Snowbound and pure and so profoundly silent that I can listen to my thoughts and longings without the interference of any judgment or ego. On each of those weeklong trips it took no more than twenty-four hours to achieve clarity and resolution. And then I spent the remaining 144 hours cold and heartsick and unable to sleep, just waiting for that return flight so I could get back to being the father of my children and the husband of my radiant, irradiating, ass-kicking wife.

Astonished by Love

Ellen Tien

—❖—

"How?" I cried as my husband lifted and carried me into the hospital bathroom, stopping to hoist my dead weight with his knee, my inert body rolling, as unpredictable and clumsy as melons in a sack. Arms dangled helplessly from my sides, someone else's arms. For a moment, mid-hoist, someone else's fingertips grazed the linoleum floor. "How can you bear to see me this way?" I asked as Will cradled and wiped and washed my paralyzed being and hauled me back to the bed. "How can you stand it?"

He laid a cool hand on my forehead, hot from the rage of corticosteroids that were rushing through my blood-stream in an attempt to bring my engorged spinal cord down to functioning dimension. "Ellen," he answered. I closed my eyes in the dark and leaned against the sound of my own name.

"I was paralyzed when I met you," he said, placing each word faceup, like a card, "and you made me whole. You showed me that it was all right to be happy. So if I have to do this every day for the rest of my life, I'll do it gladly, because you made me see that I could."

By all accounts, it was a fine marriage. Not, perhaps, a hot and heavy sort of marriage, but a fine one. Over twelve years, the number of long, moist embraces in corners and ravaged, yearning looks at breakfast certainly waned, replaced instead with trips to Whole Foods; updates on work; and sharp kicks under the table when Will forgot he wasn't supposed to mention the time the hostess, a fashion editor, had suffered a nervous breakdown and shown up to an important editorial meeting in her pajamas and slippers.

It was fine, though. We were fine. It is possible that we each sensed, in ways both acute and distant, that there might be something more out there, something thrilling and transforming. But the journey between out there and in here is formidable, and it can be difficult to navigate one's way between those two points. So we persevered, maybe without as much yearning and embracing and moistness, but we persevered with perseverance, stolid and forward facing.

We were an unlikely couple and the likeliest couple on earth. William Betts Dana was a Connecticut-born Yankee with all the rules that this implies; Ellen Jean Tien was an overachieving daughter of Chinese immigrants, with all the breaking of rules that this entails. Will Dana struggled to communicate; Ellen Tien struggled not to. Will analyzed; Ellen intuited. He let things go; she clasped them close.

Although we had known of each other in the way that anyone who pays attention to mastheads or bylines feels a kinship with those names, we officially met on a bitter winter night in 1991, at a party in a SoHo loft. He was rumpled and charmingly tongue-tied but managed to squeak out an invitation for me to visit him in Chicago, where he had recently moved. On a whim, out of a feeling of listlessness or destiny or both, I flew there and visited him. I visited him again. Then again.

On one visit, in the bargello of demi-coastal flights that would embody our courtship, we were draped on a battered brown sofa when I noticed the time on a digital clock: eleven eleven. "Quick, make a wish," I prompted.

We wished.

At eleven twelve, I asked him, "What did you wish?"

"That I could fly," he said, shrugging when a sudden laugh pricked the corners of my mouth. "It's the wish I always used to make when I was a kid. In a pinch, the words popped into my head: I wish I could fly."

This struck me as so pure and so good, I married him.

I married him, not for his looks or his money, although he had a tolerable supply of both. Nor did I marry him for his devotion or tenderness, since I was neither tender nor devoted and was unable to accept what I couldn't give back. I married him for his brains. Not for his brain, which was an altogether too complicated and tortuous arrangement of rooms with bad lighting. No, for his brains—his braininess, his kinetic body of knowledge, his vigorous intellect, his undisputable dominion over facts and theories and givens.

"Ask Will," my girlfriends would say when, in a conversation, we reached a place of puzzlement. "He knows everything."

If we were not soul mates, we were kindred spirits. We shared the religion of language, a belief in words and the strength of their composition. He was an editor and I was a writer, and we became each other's eyes. He read every piece I wrote. His were the eyes I turned to first; his were the brains I relied upon.

More than that, he had a greater faith in me than anyone else had ever mustered—greater even than my parents', deeper even than my son's. He maintained an unflagging confidence in my abilities, real or imagined: Whenever a discussion arose that involved any type of high-functioning career, he invariably gestured toward me and enthused.

"You would make the greatest Supreme Court judge."

"You would be the best medical examiner ever."

"They should hire you to run the *New Yorker.*"

Once, after he had declared that I would make an exemplary prime minister, I pointed out that he always said that I would be the best such and such and, frankly, it seemed a bit indiscriminate. "Untrue," he protested. "I've never said you would make the best underwater tunnel digger."

That's where he was mistaken. Before we met, I was one of the greatest sandhogs of our time.

But if the Man Who Knew Everything believed I could do anything, then maybe I would have to believe it, too.

We bought an apartment on Twenty-second Street.

We adopted a dog who looked like a fox.

We had a son.

We used to joke that the arc of our life would move from "Did the dog poop?" to "Did the baby poop?" to "Did you poop?" and then—finished. Done. A complete life together, charted in three easy-to-answer questions.

Except that somewhere between the baby pooping and me pooping—June 17, 2002, to be precise—I got cancer.

Now I grant you, when you're already six pages in, cancer can be rather a bomb to drop on a story, especially when it serves only as more exposition and is really somewhat beside the point. Allow me to detonate: I was diagnosed with breast cancer; it was small and intense and manageable.

Of course, when I say *manageable*, I mean by me. At the ping of diagnosis, Will's busy brains etiolated into vapor. It wasn't that he couldn't cope—it was that he wouldn't. My girlfriends went with me to doctor consultations; my best friend, Jacquie, accompanied me to my surgery. My surgeon, Dr. Nowak, assumed that I was a single mother. I am pretty sure that my oncologist, Dr. Tepler, thought I was a lesbian. The former had referred me to the latter, and I pictured the two physicians, running into one another at breast cancer conferences, exchanging small talk.

"By the way, I've started treating that patient of yours, Ellen Tien."

"Oh, right—the single lesbian mother?"

When my radiation treatments began—eight A.M. appointments at Weill Cornell's Stich Radiation Center—Will officially took his bolt of denial to the tailor and had it made into a three-piece suit.

"Look at you, all dressed and ready to go," he would say gaily on a Monday morning (he is a morning person in the worst way). "Where are you headed?"

"Radiation," I would say.

Tuesday: "Where are you off to on such a nice morning?"

"Radiation," I would answer darkly.

Wednesday: "What are you—?"

"Radiation!"

It was the same for six weeks.

But if there is a gist to this part of the story—and I am a terrific fan of the gist—it is that in a marriage, what seems like a brute transgression on the outside can transliterate to merely a workaday blemish on the inside. The gander's indolence or neglect might appall the flock but may barely register with the goose.

If I couldn't quite commit to forgiving Will for his absenteeism, I could, in a specialized way, get it—or at least I would have to say I did unless I was willing to play the fool who stayed with the fool who played her for a fool. Getting it was the toothpick that could save the card house, the international symbol for truce. How many times had I oppugned Will for a perceived disregard (a forgotten quart of milk, a veiled insult from a member of his family) only to be neutralized: Okay. Okay. I get it.

So the business of living went on as usual, although now slightly hobbled by the realization that life was no longer a simple matter of three poop questions. But since the evolution of a relationship is less about forgiveness and scatology and more about the accumulation of real estate, we forged onward and bought a weekend house in the jungles of Connecticut. For the next year, we excitedly huddled together in the glow of a collective project, connected by the inherent promise found in paint chips and carpet swatches and fixtures.

It was Memorial Day weekend 2004, our first weekend in the new house, and we were in an Ace Hardware store when the magma burst loose and Pompeii was buried.

A crushing pain blossomed cruelly in my chest and my back—I staggered back between the spools of chain-link and the bags of peat moss and knew instantly that something was wrong. We made a dash for the car and drove to a hospital in nearby Torrington. I remember Will tersely counting down the miles.

Only seven more miles to go.

Only six more miles to go.

I doubled over in my seat, negotiating for air. I started to lose feeling in my fingers and toes. At one point, I turned and looked in the backseat and saw my son—his chubby six-year-old hands clenched in fear, tears silently streaming down his face—mumbling to himself, "Don't make a sound. Don't get in the way. Don't make a sound. Don't get in the way."

I think that was the worst part of all.

Only four more miles to go.

We arrived at the hospital in Torrington, the morphine was plugged in, the bottom dropped out of reality, and I stopped being able to chronicle the events in any organized fashion. At some juncture, the chief neurologist walked in the room and declared herself "completely unqualified to diagnose the problem," which was reassuring. There was talk of airlifting me back to New York, but doctors were concerned that the paralysis would spread to my lungs and they would not be able to intubate me in midair, so an ambulance was deemed preferable. Will's cousin Kate picked up our son so Will could ride with me.

By the time we raced past Westchester, I was paralyzed from the shoulders down.

When we pulled into the ambulance entrance of Weill Cornell Medical Center on Seventieth Street, I remember Will musing, "Wow—we made really good time."

The doctors—these being rather more qualified than the ones in Torrington—swiftly arrived at a diagnosis: acute transverse myelitis, a rare idiopathic condition in which a body's immune system attacks the myelin sheath around its own spinal cord. It was unrelated to the cancer, a second fluke, a brilliant stroke of unluck.

I was assigned the top myelitis specialist in the city, Dr. Apatoff, a wiry man in a bow tie with a hyper-intelligent face and the bedside manner of a schnauzer.

There were high-dose IV steroids and MRIs and spinal taps and more steroids.

The IV tree grew thicker and thicker with bags. There were drugs to calm the drugs that inflamed and other drugs to calm the calming drugs and then new drugs to counteract the over-calmingness of the drugs before them. The narcotics dogs chased their tails up and down my veins until my mind was burned into the blue-white burst of a flashbulb, all heat and muffled explosions and floating spots.

I remember weakly joking to Will, "What next? Thrush?"

The next day, I got thrush.

A few days after that, steroid-induced edema blew me up like a human blister. In seventy-two hours, I gained forty pounds of water weight; as the fluid rushed into my face, my eyelid and the right side of my nose—weakened by a host of secondary infections—collapsed in a heap somewhere above my mouth.

I was no longer presentable or sane, yet a throng of visitors persisted in making my room a ruthless party, the strange manic gaiety of which pushed me deeper into confusion.

Food and flowers formed a slag heap along the windows.

I was afraid to sleep alone in the room.

My stomach, bruised from daily multiple injections, turned the deep, mottled maroon of a tortoise cowry.

My friend Elizabeth baked an enormous pink buttercream cake.

I snapped at Will in front of his mother, and the next day when she called—a nurse propped the phone on a pillow next to my ear—the whole room could hear her anxiously wailing, "You must be nicer to Willie! You *must* be nicer to Willie!"

"Sheesh," someone in the room said. "Pick your priorities."

Everyone laughed.

My son went to a carnival, and I worried that he might horse around during a ride and lean too far one way and his body would be crushed between the metal cars.

Jacquie brought me a Porthault bathrobe and I wept because I bled on it.

I asked Will repeatedly if the dog missed me.

Time stacked atop time. I was moved out of the ICU, first into the neurological ward and then upstairs to a grimly cheerful physical rehab unit called Baker 17 that had a shiny Pergo wood laminate floor, peevish nurses, and orderlies who flatly refused to change sheets.

Two weeks later, Will and I came home with a wheelchair and walker.

Three months later, I could walk on my own but had no sensation down the left side of my body.

Nine months later, Will drove me to the office of Dr. Daniel Baker, a plastic surgeon, who painstakingly began to give me back my self, reconstructing my face in a series of surgeries, each four months apart. After the first surgery, in which my collapsed face was fattened with cartilage grafts, my nose foreshortened and upturned, I looked like a pig. After the second surgery, I looked like exactly half a pig. This was all according to plan.

At the one-year mark, the function in my hands had improved, but I had no use of my thumbs or my right index finger.

I still can't tie a shoe or write legibly or play the piano.

"How?" I asked Will as he bathed and dressed and fed me for weeks upon weeks, matter-of-factly and without complaint, as if this had always been the arrangement.

"How can you bear to see me this way?" I asked him as

he laid ice packs across the stitches around my nose; cleaned the brittle, bloody lacquer pooled behind my ears, which had been pillaged for cartilage; tried—oh, how he tried in his clumsy, ignorant, manlike way!—to help me brush my hair or fasten jewelry or even put on makeup in a grotesquely comic attempt to simulate a regular human face.

For the better part of a year, I declined all but the most obligatory social events. Subjecting my distorted, crumpled features and bloated girth to public gaze was too awful to be borne: the startled expressions, the quick aversion of eyes, the way that people I had known for years no longer recognized me.

He never averted his eyes.

"How can you stand it?" I asked him, when he came home from work at night, only to have to tackle an additional mountain of accrued tasks: the mail to open, books to put away, printers to fill, food to warm, buttons to unbutton, presents to wrap. I once relied on his eyes, his brains. Now I needed his hands, too.

He started bringing me scissors—sewing shears, meat scissors, paper cutters, clippers with specially designed handles, spring-loaded cutters—until I found a pair that I could operate. He bought me fat magic markers that I could grasp in my fist. Every morning he unscrewed bottles of water, de-foiled cups of yogurt, opened cartons of milk, and then closed them up and put them back in the refrigerator so I could have access to them later. All this he did without fanfare or comment. All this he did so I wouldn't always have to feel stranded.

This is not a story about how crisis can rejuvenate love or whisk us to new heights or strengthen and improve a relationship. Sometimes it does and sometimes it doesn't, but more often than not it eventually just blends in like paint, stroked smoother and longer and wider, until it disappears into the plain—remembered but not perceived. The landscape reverts to sameness. In a society that exalts the special and the different, do we dare to posit that sameness may be our salvation?

There is fortitude in something that has always stood.

Marriage is sameness. It is a contraption, at times creakier than others, with a discrete set of ropes and pulleys that two partners pass back and forth until they can no longer. It is a fabric with a fixed set of threads weaving in and out of the patterns, showing up here, then showing up there again. The fibers weave sameness, the very sameness that impels some people to divorce, others to mate for life.

I will never make a complete recovery. This is a hard sentence to say, an even harder sentence to write. But this is not a story about me. This is the story of a marriage, a marriage that granted, in every state of change, sameness. A marriage that, when people asked, "How are things?" allowed me to answer, "The same."

By all accounts, it has been a fine marriage. It saw two big bumps but it has seen even more paved road. And so Will and I continue to pass the same ropes back and forth, to follow the same finite set of threads as they disappear and return.

It is a fine marriage. We are fine. It is possible that we once sensed, in ways both acute and distant, that there might be something more out there, something thrilling and transforming, but now we know that we were wrong.

The Family You Choose

It's the ones you can call up at four A.M. that matter.

–Marlene Dietrich

There Were No Words

Elizabeth Strout

The place had wooden tables, their thick tops shiny from years of use, and the floors were wooden, too, and shone like honey. There must have been sun coming through the high windows, because I remember light falling on the table that held our cups of coffee and maybe our food. It was lunchtime. I must have ordered food, but I can't remember what it was. My friend Kathy sat across from me, waiting. We both taught at the college nearby, and earlier I had told her that something awful was happening that I needed to talk to her about.

What was happening was so painful that I had written down the words. I couldn't speak them out loud. I, who was such a talkative person that I had sometimes been teased about falling asleep talking, waking up talking, talking even as I floated face down with a snorkel in my mouth on some Caribbean blue sea, pointing out a fish to my daughter—I, who had been known to "say anything," literally could not give voice to what was happening, my terror was that deep, and so I had written down the words. Kathy's hands I can still see, spread patiently on the table, and the silver rings she wore.

I was thirty-six, what they call a lifetime ago.

These days I often find myself thinking of the Edna St. Vincent Millay poem "Childhood Is the Kingdom Where Nobody Dies." I think how it means that childhood is the kingdom where there is someplace still safe, and how up until that day when I sat across from Kathy, I was still in the kingdom where marriages were safe and where, in spite of private disappointments and difficult accommodations sometimes made, loyalty reigned, where treachery might peer in a window but not come in.

Later—oh, months and months, years later—I would actually feel glad to have gone through this, to understand more fully the complications of love and accountability and sadness and healing; I would be glad later for all I had a chance to learn, but that day as I sat across from Kathy, the sunlight hitting the honey-wood table, and as I pushed toward her the small piece of paper on which I had written words that made my heart crack, I was dimly aware that I was stepping into a river on whose banks I might never stand again.

And here is what I remember most: Kathy finished reading my words, and wordlessly tears fell from her eyes. That is the gift my friend handed me that day. Kathy's wordless tears of empathy, a friend so generous that she wept for me. Childhood is the kingdom where nobody dies. Where marriages are safe. I left the banks of childhood then, and Kathy's tears were like hands reaching for me as I, stunned, afraid of drowning in the river of grown-up land, struggled to the other side.

Female Friendship Never Gets Old

Elizabeth Kelsey

When I first glimpsed Murdina at a party, the word that came to mind was *grand*. Tall and curvy, with massive jewelry, she was confident yet unintimidating. In her charming New Zealand accent, she complimented my hair, and soon we were talking about her divorce, the boyfriend she saw once every few weeks, and the fact that she had never gotten around to having children. I told her I felt no urge, either.

She was forty-nine. I was twenty-nine and had just moved back home to Tallahassee with my boyfriend. Paul had given me plenty of reasons to leave, like the time he grabbed my arm hard in the middle of an argument, or the time he called me stupid. Still, he was my first love—and

I couldn't bring myself to end the relationship. Instead, I started spending less time with him and more with Murdina.

Sundays, I'd meet her for brunch after my morning run, and she'd be waiting at our favorite table. She'd tell me about her ex-husband, for whom she'd emigrated to Florida (when she said his name, George, she scrunched her nose as though she'd smelled something bad), and her job as head of a state government agency. I'd tell her about whatever race I was training for. Murdina was kind but sharp-tongued: Piss her off and you might become the "festering carbuncle" or "narcissistic Nancy." When I told her about Paul's controlling behavior, she named him TD—short for Tiny Dick—which diminished his power over me the next time he raised his voice.

One night Paul didn't come home until four A.M. The next day I called Murdina and asked, "Can I come stay with you?"

A night became eight months. We turned her former garage into a bedroom and decorated it with elephant-patterned curtains. Lying in bed, I'd clutch Murdina's twenty-pound tortoiseshell cat to my chest and cry. The next morning, over breakfast, Murdina would remind me, "That man has the emotional intelligence of a frozen pea."

Our life together began to follow a comfortable pattern. Before work we'd have coffee with her neighbor Ed, an octogenarian who mowed his lawn in cowboy boots. Then we'd climb into the Blue Beast, her ancient Chevrolet Cavalier, and she'd drop me off at my job as a copywriter. Saturdays, she'd take me to lunch with her friends, most of them college professors or CEOs she'd met during their midlife divorces. Soon they were counseling me on my "mini divorce." When I called Paul an a-hole, they laughed, assuring me, "You'll meet another a-hole."

When I turned thirty and Murdina fifty, we celebrated our "eightieth" birthday with the large social group we'd cultivated. In a gold Badgley Mischka dress, standing beside Murdina, I felt as though I actually glowed. I'd had close friendships before, but this was different. Murdina was more stable and self-aware than my younger friends, and without spouses or children, we'd had time to invest in each other. She'd confessed that her feelings toward me were initially maternal, but that she'd soon realized she just enjoyed my company. It was as though we were in one of those "Boston marriages" I'd learned about in American lit: two nineteenth-century women who lived together and supported each other, financially and emotionally, without a man.

As the months passed, I thought less and less about Paul and more about myself. About a year after I left Murdina's, I met Maroun, who was respectful, doting, and fun. Even Murdina agreed—after careful scrutiny—that he was "a gem." I asked her to be the maid of honor at our wedding.

It was Murdina, after all, who had taught me what I wanted in a marriage.

Oprah and Gayle, Uncensored

Lisa Kogan

In 2006, Lisa Kogan, O, The Oprah Magazine's *longtime writer at large, sat down to plumb the depths of a legendary friendship. The result: an interview for the ages.*

What?" Oprah asks as Gayle plucks at a wisp of her pal's hair.

"I miss the curls," Gayle answers.

"Gayle doesn't like my hair," Oprah tells me. "But that's okay, 'cause I do."

"So you're allowed to criticize each other's looks?" I venture.

"Sure," Gayle says. "I tried growing out my bangs a few months ago, and Oprah hated it."

"Yeah," Oprah says, "but then I thought, 'Hey, I don't have to sleep with her.'"

And so it begins . . .

LISA: Funny you should say that. Every time I tell somebody I'm interviewing Oprah and Gayle, the response is the same: "Huh. Are they, you know, together?"

OPRAH: People are still saying that?

LISA: Every single person. I say, "No, I don't think so." And they respond with something like, "You're very naive."

OPRAH: I understand why people think we're gay. There isn't a definition in our culture for this kind of bond between women. I get why people have to label it—how can you be this close without it being sexual? How else can you explain a level of intimacy where someone *always* loves you, *always* respects you, *always* admires you?

GAYLE: If we were gay, we would so tell you.

OPRAH: And for people to still be asking—that means they think I'm a liar. That bothers me.

GAYLE: Particularly given how open you've been about everything else in your life.

OPRAH: I've told nearly everything there is to tell. My stuff is out there. People think I'd be so ashamed of being gay that I wouldn't admit it? Oh, please.

LISA: Do the rumors bother you, Gayle?

GAYLE: Not anymore, but I used to say, "Oprah, you have to do something. It's hard enough for me to get a date on a Saturday night."

OPRAH: We were in the Bahamas—I was giving a wedding for my niece. We were having a big party in my suite and who comes walking in—

GAYLE: With my suitcase.

OPRAH: With her suitcase! And I knew what everybody was thinking: "They're gay. Has to be, because Stedman isn't around."

GAYLE: The tabloid headline was OPRAH'S HIDEAWAY WITH GAL PAL. Ridiculous. [*Pause*] But that said, if Oprah were a man, I *would* marry her.

OPRAH: The truth is, no matter where I am, whether Stedman is there or not, Gayle's in the other room.

GAYLE: If Stedman didn't accept me, it would be very difficult.

OPRAH: See, that would never be a question for me. If you don't like my best friend, you don't like me. That's not negotiable. Smoking is nonnegotiable. Not liking my best friend—forget it! [*Laughter*]

LISA: Oprah, how did you feel when Gayle got married?

OPRAH: I was a little sad, mostly because I didn't think it was going to work out.

GAYLE: You never told me that.

OPRAH: It just didn't feel joyful. You know how you go to weddings and they're full of joy?

GAYLE: You didn't think it was going to work out *at the wedding*?

OPRAH: There are weddings you go to and you're just filled with all this hope for the couple. I didn't feel that at yours.

GAYLE: But you were my maid of honor!

OPRAH: I never told you because it wasn't my place to.

GAYLE: I wouldn't have believed you anyway.

OPRAH: No. Also I felt maybe it's just me being jealous. Maybe I'm worried our friendship will change. But it didn't.

LISA: What about when you had a baby, Gayle?

GAYLE: Nothing changed between us. Oprah was there. She came shortly after Kirby was born and then right after Will was born. She was *there*.

OPRAH: My gift to her was a full-time nanny.

GAYLE: Right. The kids are eleven months apart, and Oprah goes, "I got you the perfect gift." I'm thinking, *Oh good, a double stroller.* But the gift turned out to be a nanny! She said, "I'll pay the nanny's salary for as long as you feel you need her."

OPRAH: She kept that nanny for eight years. But even as a working-outside-the-home mom, she was always there to put her kids to bed. She said, "I want mine to be the first face my kids see when they wake up and the last before they go to sleep." So it wasn't like the nanny—

GAYLE: Replaced me.

OPRAH: I admire a lot about Gayle. But when I think about the way she raised her kids, I get weepy.

GAYLE: Why weepy? That's surprising to me.

OPRAH: Maybe I haven't said it to you very often, but I say it to others all the time. Gayle is the best mother I have ever known. She is 100 percent there for her kids. We'll be on the phone, in the middle of a conversation, and the kids will enter the room, and everything stops. This just happened last week, and her son's nineteen. She goes, "Hi, Willser. You got your Willser face on. Mommy loves you. Good morning, Bear. Hi, Kirby-Cakes." She stops the conversation to greet them and let them know they've been seen and heard. They've grown up with such love and support from Gayle, *and* from her ex-husband. She understood that though the marriage was over, her husband still needed to maintain a strong relationship with his kids. That takes a real woman.

GAYLE: Years ago, when Oprah was thinking of leaving her show, she said, "You should move to Chicago, and we'll incorporate you into the show. And then at the end of the year, I'll pass the baton to you—but you'd have to move to Chicago." And I said, "I can't do that because Billy wouldn't be able to see the kids on a regular basis."

OPRAH: I said, "Do you realize what I'm offering?"

GAYLE: And I go, "Yeah, I do." But the kids were young, so I just said, "No, I can't."

OPRAH: That's why she's the best, and so are her kids.

They're my godchildren. There are shots of me crawling around on all fours with Kirby, playing horsey and stuff. I remember when William first came to my farm: He was running around saying, "Auntie O, you have a pool *and* a wacuzzi? Can you afford all this?" He was little, little, little, and I had all these antique Shaker boxes. He was stacking 'em like—

GAYLE: Blocks.

OPRAH: And knocking 'em over. I went, "William! Put those boxes down!" These kids weren't used to anybody raising their voice—they were never spanked or yelled at. So he was like, wacuzzi or no wacuzzi, I'm outta here. He told his mommy, "I want to go home." The kids made a lot of noise, and they had all kinds of bright yellow plastic things everywhere. And the TV was on and the same video was always playing over and over. But Gayle helped me adjust.

GAYLE: I'm always taken aback when Oprah talks about me and the kids because a lot of mothers feel about their children the way I do about mine.

OPRAH: But they don't always have kids who turn out the way yours have. Everybody wants to raise good people, not just smart people who go to Ivy League schools. But you have to be a good person to raise good people.

LISA: Do you two talk every day?

GAYLE: Usually three or four times a day.

OPRAH: Then there's my night call. When she was on vacation with her sisters, and we hadn't had a conversation, I realized I felt far more stressed. I've never had a day's therapy, but I have my night chats with Gayle.

GAYLE: We talk about everything and anything. It's been that way since the beginning.

OPRAH: The first time Gayle spent the night at my house there was a snowstorm and she couldn't get home. She was a production assistant, and I was the six o'clock anchor in Baltimore.

GAYLE: Anchors and PAs do not socialize—newsroom hierarchy.

OPRAH: But I said, "You can stay at my house." The next day, we went to the mall.

GAYLE: Remember Casual Corner? They had those two-for-$19.99 sales.

OPRAH: I ended up buying two sweaters.

GAYLE: I called my mother and said, "You know my friend Oprah? She bought *two* sweaters!" I was into layaway back then, for one sweater. [*Laughter*]

OPRAH: Years later, for my forty-second birthday, we were in Miami, and I decided I was going to buy myself a present. On the way to the mall, we passed a car dealership where I spotted a black Bentley. I'm like, "That is the most beautiful car." So we pulled over and I bought that Bentley on the spot. I said to Gayle, "This is a Casual Corner moment." And she was like, "You're going to buy that now? Shouldn't you think about it or at least try to negotiate a better deal?" I said, "Gayle, that's what you said when I bought the two sweaters."

LISA: What's that Paul Simon lyric? *After changes upon changes, we are more or less the same.*

OPRAH: One of my favorite moments was about ten, twelve years ago when we were in Racine, Wisconsin. We're in a traffic jam because everyone was headed to the concert hall where I was speaking, and Gayle says, "Where are all these people going?" We pull up to the venue, and Gayle goes, "What's going on here?"

GAYLE: The cops were lined up, double rows.

OPRAH: Gayle's going, "Who's here? Who's here?" I go, "I am, you nitwit!"

GAYLE: "You mean all these people are coming to see you?" I could not believe it.

LISA: Gayle, when you started at *O*, did either of you worry that working for Oprah might change the dynamic between you?

GAYLE: I wasn't worried. But people did say, "You should *never* work with your friend."

OPRAH: That's how I know people don't understand this relationship, because other people's definition of *friend* isn't what ours is. One time I was doing a show about when your best friend sleeps with your husband. The ultimate betrayal. That is not possible in this relationship.

GAYLE: What I know for sure: I will never sleep with Stedman.

OPRAH: What did you used to say? "If you ever find me in the bed with Stedman—"

GAYLE: "Don't even be mad. Just scoop me up and get me to a hospital, because you will know I'm very ill."

OPRAH: "Carry me tenderly out the door." [*Laughter*]

GAYLE: But people do ask, "How can you work for a friend?" I can because I know the magazine is called *O*. The bottom line is, somebody has to have the final word. Oprah's not right all the time, but her record is pretty damn good. Which is not to say you can't disagree with her.

OPRAH: That's why Gayle's so great for me at the magazine—she almost always has exactly the opinion I do. But when she doesn't agree, she'll fight for her point as though there were a *G* on that magazine. We have "disagree," and we have "strongly disagree." If Gayle strongly, strongly feels something about somebody—

GAYLE: It gives her pause.

OPRAH: It gives me pause, because Gayle's been my— she's apple pie and Chevrolet. She loves everybody. So if there's somebody she doesn't like, that gets my attention because she's truly everybody's friend—far friendlier than I am.

GAYLE: I'm very social.

OPRAH: I'm not social. Nor am I all that friendly.

GAYLE: All Oprah needs is a good book.

LISA: So I'm hearing about differences. What are the similarities?

GAYLE: We became friends that first night because I'd never before met somebody I felt was like me. Certainly not another black girl. I grew up in an all-white community. I remember getting embarrassed in fourth grade when a boy in my class said, "If it weren't for Abraham Lincoln, you'd be my slave." I still remember that. Oprah and I had the same sensibilities. We liked the same music. We thought smart—

OPRAH: Smart and articulate—

GAYLE: Was not a bad thing.

OPRAH: We were the only black girls in our schools, and I was the only black girl I knew who loved Neil Diamond.

GAYLE: I liked Barry Manilow.

LISA: You guys were made for each other.

OPRAH: [*Laughter*] It's that whole being-the-odd-girl-out thing—we didn't fit in to everybody else's perception of what it's like to be a black girl.

GAYLE: But we still had a very strong sense of being black and were very proud of being black. So to meet another black girl like that was, wow! And we were the same age, we were both single—we just immediately bonded.

OPRAH: But she was clearly upper middle class, and I was clearly from a very poor background. Gayle had a pool growing up!

GAYLE: I had a swimming pool, a maid. We grew up very, very well.

OPRAH: She had a maid. My mother *was* a maid. You know what I'm saying? I'd never met a black person with a maid. It was like, "Lord, really? At your house?"

GAYLE: So we became friends right away, and we've been friends ever since.

LISA: Gayle, has Oprah ever said anything about you on the air that inadvertently crossed the privacy line?

GAYLE: Well, there was the time she said I pooped all over the table during childbirth. People stopped me on the street after that one.

OPRAH: In retrospect, I might have thought a little more before mentioning that. But I was talking about pregnancy, what actually happens—and that's one of the things people never tell you. She goes, "Well, listen–"

GAYLE: "Next time you're talking about shitting on a table, keep my name out of it!" I was a news anchor by then: "I'm Gayle King, *Eyewitness News.*" And I'd get people saying, "Yes, I saw you on the news–I didn't know you pooped all over." [*Laughter*]

LISA: Let's stay on body stuff for a second. My best friend and I have a pact: If something ever happens to one of us, whoever's still mobile has to come by every three weeks and pluck any unseemly facial hair.

OPRAH: We don't have that pact because it would happen automatically.

GAYLE: My only instructions have been to go get her journals.

LISA: And if something happens to you?

GAYLE: I would just always want her to be involved in my children's lives.

OPRAH: Her children are my children. There's nothing I wouldn't do for her, there's nothing she wouldn't do for me. There is a line of respect that is unspoken, on both our parts. I remember once when

Gayle came to my house: I was already making a lot of money, and she wasn't. And we discovered I had $422 in my pocket.

GAYLE: $482.

OPRAH: Okay, $482.

GAYLE: But who's counting?

OPRAH: I had $482 just sort of stuck into a coat pocket.

GAYLE: In your pants pocket. You know how sometimes you just find a five? Or a twenty is like, whoo! She pulls out $482.

OPRAH: Okay, you tell the story.

GAYLE: I'd gotten to Chicago on a Super Saver ticket—you know, back when you had to buy thirty days in advance for a decent price. She was living in Chicago, and I was married, and we had scrimped—I remember that once Billy and I didn't have ten dollars to go to the movies. He was in law school and I was the only one working. So for her to pull out $482 was like, wow! She goes, "God, where'd this come from? You want it?" And I went, "Oh, no. No. I'm good. I'm fine." But I'm thinking, "God, that would pay the light bill, the phone bill, the gas bill."

And she just puts it back. It's probably still in that damn pocket. She was just extending a gesture, just being nice: "Oh, you want it?"

OPRAH: But years later, she said, "You remember that time you pulled out the $482?"

GAYLE: I said, "I wanted that money so bad!"

OPRAH: "I needed that money so bad, but I wouldn't take it." You know what that's like? It's incredible for somebody like me who lives in a world where everybody wants a piece of you—people feel they deserve a piece of you. Strangers think that.

GAYLE: Now I happily accept all gifts. [*Laughter*] No, but it just wouldn't have felt right.

OPRAH: She's never asked me for a dime. There is a level of mutual respect that comes from being with somebody who doesn't want anything from you but you. There will never be an ulterior motive. I have to say, it would have been a much different relationship had she taken the money. In a real friendship, you have to be equals.

GAYLE: Not necessarily financial equals.

OPRAH: No, but equal in respect. I can't put myself in a position where I need you to do things for me, or expect you to do things for me with strings attached. But let me also say that the person who has the money has to have a generous spirit. Early on, when I started to make a lot of money and we'd go shopping, I'd say, "Look, the deal is if you see something you really want, I'll get it. I don't want to play this, 'No, no, no, you don't have to buy that for me,' because I'm really willing to get it for you." I do that now with all my friends. But what you don't want is a situation where the person always expects that you'll be the one to pay. Nobody wants to be seen as an ATM.

LISA: You want connection. Someone who doesn't have an agenda.

OPRAH: Absolutely. So in a way, our friendship is better than a marriage or a sexual relationship. There's no such thing as unconditional love in a marriage as far as I'm concerned, 'cause let me tell you, there are some conditions. [*Laughter*] So don't ask me to give you unconditional love because there are certain things I won't tolerate. But in this friendship, there isn't a label, there isn't a definition of what it's supposed to be.

LISA: Do you ever think about the inevitable—about who's going first?

GAYLE: I think about when we get old, but I can't imagine life without Oprah. I'll go first if I can be ninety and you can be ninety-one.

OPRAH: Something about this relationship feels otherworldly to me, like it was designed by a power and a hand greater than my own. Whatever our friendship is, it's been a very fun ride.

The Witches

Patricia Volk

Four women. One leafy urban park. Topics: men, wrinkles, headlines, coffee, one another.

The phone rings at seven on the dot. It's Frances Kiernan, writer.

"Are we on?" she trills.

"Mm-hmm."

I call Molly Haskell, the film critic.

"We're on," I say.

Molly calls Lily Tuck, another writer.

At seven thirty (weather permitting) we meet in Central Park, Tuesdays and Thursdays, like a religion.

By seven thirty Frannie has scoured the *Times*. She fills us in on anything incendiary. We talk about our work, we talk about our wrinkles, we talk about our men: current, ex, and late. We talk about our editors, our agents, what we've read, what we've heard, what we did last night. We laugh our heads off.

One of us has a good ear. We walk on that side of her. One of us has a propensity for surgery. We slow down for her. One of us has a new apartment in Paris. Her, we miss.

We peel out of the park at Eighty-fifth and head for cappuccino at Le Pain Quotidien. We take turns paying. Molly keeps track on a little pad she is rarely without. If somehow we're not sure whose turn it is, we shoot for it, as in "The odd finger is it!" I understood in a newly profound way what it meant for Lily to have grown up in Europe, because shooting was news to her.

A couple of times a year, my power-broker friend Michael reserves the best table for us at Elio's and we get swanked up and meet for dinner. We never fail to be shocked by how beautiful we are with makeup. It was at one of these dinners that a famous older man and his hilariously young sweetie pie were cooing at the table next to us. We gossiped fiendishly. The next day, we opened the papers and something terrible had happened to the man.

"We're witches," Frannie declared. Now we call ourselves the Witches. I'm the self-proclaimed Alpha Witch because I've been going around the reservoir the longest and I started the thing, and I'm the fastest, although Lily, who is accustomed to being best, says she is.

I love everything about the Witches. I love that we are wildly, wickedly different except for the fact that we all write and have good manners. Molly is Southern. Frannie is old New York courtly. Lily is international. Molly dresses like Huck Finn by day and Doris Day by night. Lily, even in spandex, looks like Greta Garbo. Our points of view couldn't be more different. Like the park, we're unpredictable; we keep changing.

By eight forty-five we're back at our computers, ready to rock 'n' roll. The walk is 1.67 miles, or 3,677 steps, according to my pedometer. (Molly wrote the brand down in her little book, and now she wears a pedometer, too.) One loop takes us thirty minutes. That's 3.34 miles per hour, or almost as fast as the fastest cockroach in the world, *Periplaneta americana*. If there's a better way to start the day, I'm all ears.

We are the Witches, hear us cackle.

With Friends Like Me,
Who Needs Strangers?

Amy Dickinson

The letter arrived just after Christmas. It was from Mary, my post-college roommate and dear friend. "I know that I have said or done something that upset you, and I am so sorry," she'd written. She'd also sent a little notebook decorated with cowgirls on the cover. She knew I would love it, and she was right.

Mary and I had last seen each other about six months before, when I took a business trip to her hometown of Atlanta. We spent a morning together, having coffee and browsing in vintage shops. Since then she had called twice, and I hadn't gotten back to her. A new job; a move from Washington, D.C., to Chicago; pressing duties as a mother, daughter, and sister—I'd had my share of excuses for not being in touch with Mary and a score of other friends.

Just as a moth encases herself in a frosty shell, I had been tucking myself away from the people who know me best. And by not making the effort to stay close, I'd given some of my friends the impression that I'd left the relationship altogether. I'd recently received plaintive e-mails and messages from them: *Where are you? I haven't heard from you in a long time!* I knew that my friends would make this effort for a while, and then they would give up.

Mary's note was the mortifying last straw.

When I lived in proximity to my friends, our regular in-person contact fed me. I'd run into them at my child's school or at the store. We'd have impromptu coffee and conversations. The fact that I wasn't very good at initiating contact was obscured by the fact that I was always colliding with someone I'd been meaning (but not managing) to call.

Moving halfway across the country exposed my weakness. I kept waiting to bump into a pal at the market, and I never did. I kept waiting for the perfect time to get in touch, and it never came.

And now the thought that my inertia caused a dear

friend to question herself made me want to weep. So here's what I decided to do: I began to fix my friendships, one by one. Not by being a perfect friend—I may never manage to send birthday cards or remember their favorite lipstick shade—but by being a good enough friend, honestly acknowledging my failings. I decided to contact one each day, either by e-mail or phone, just to say hello. I would master the check-in call.

I was holding on to Mary's *What did I do wrong?* note when I reached her on her cell phone. "You want to know what you did wrong?" I asked. "You decided to be friends with me, and I am such a jackass!"

We laughed. That's how we fixed it. And now I get to start again.

It's All Relative

Family is the home we carry inside us.

–O EDITORS

What Betty Knows

Monica Wood

In the beginning, she was my big sister: three years older, a head taller, and—I knew even then—not like the rest of us. As I grew up, she became my little sister, whom I protected from mean boys, the neighbor's heartless crow, and the word *retard*. She became literally littler, too: Today the fluffy top of her head barely grazes my shoulder, and I'm no giant myself.

When people ask about Betty's "mental age," I never know what to say. We're in our fifties now, shaped by the slings and arrows of fortune both outrageous and ordinary. The gap in our physical age broadens as her teeth loosen and her bones crumble; but the intellectual chasm that divides us, once so obvious and immutable, widens and narrows in startling ways. Betty can't write a grocery list or read a thermometer, but she can take the temperature of a room better than anyone I know. She can't reliably feed a cat or lock a door, but if you tell her a secret she'll keep it for a hundred years.

Betty calls her best friend, Laura, by her full name, a vaguely Victorian quirk that Laura mimics, because in certain tight circles Betty is the last word on etiquette and all else. Weekdays at three sharp, the phone rings.

"Hi, Betty Wood."

"Hi, Laura Ellis."

"What did you have for snack, Betty Wood?"

"Twinkie, Laura Ellis. You?"

"Twinkie, Betty Wood."

This is the After Work Call, following their shift at a sheltered workshop they refer to as "the shop." They've been at it for thirty years, pleasant hours sanding blocks, potting seedlings, or sorting secondhand clothes. Side by side they work (Laura with her telltale Down-syndrome silhouette: soft as a snow-muffled shrub, her round tongue resting on her lower lip like a winterberry. Betty, by contrast, is composed of points and angles, like a bird in a children's book: You could draw a decent likeness in a few sharp strokes). They chat and jabber from first bell to last, because the shop, like any workplace, teems with intrigue. Stolen boyfriends, hoarded candy, shifting alliances and dibs on lunch seats, the occasional dustup or medical crisis, the full operatic range of human striving.

Betty is the watcher, her pale eyes seeming to take in every contingency at once. If there's peace to be made, she will make it. If not, she's quick to step out of the way. "I'm a good lady," she tells whoever will listen, and I doubt that anyone to date has disagreed.

Because Betty thrives on routine, her week recycles the same highlight reel. Saturday-morning infomercials, Tuesday lunch out, Thursday paycheck ($3); but the jewel in the crown is Friday night, when she beelines to Laura's house to laugh it up with Ron, Laura's adored and adorable old father. Because we lost our parents young, and then our beloved aunt and uncle, Betty has perfected the art of choosing surrogates. Ron—whom Betty calls "Fella"—makes their weekly lemon pie, a sacrosanct step-by-step that Betty hawkishly supervises, setting out utensils that her pushover host allows her to store according to her own unknowable logic. In a whip-quick sleight of hand, she plucks a measuring cup from a toy chest, and there ensues a great cloud of flour and much pan-rattling and conventional disaster—the dog gulps up half the filling on a good day, all of it on a great one—but somehow a pie results, a foamy treasure they can crow over.

Then Ron falls ill, and the trappings of pie-making give way to the trappings of something else. Pill bottles line the counter. Apron strings wrap twice around his ebbing waist. And finally no more pie; instead a hospital bed hogs the parlor, a sobering meringue of fluffed pillows and daisy-yellow sheets.

"Does she get it?" people ask. Which leaves me speechless.

Betty gets hospital beds. She gets soup by the thimble-ful. She gets syringes in the fridge. She can spot, sooner than most, the signposts on that one-way road.

And she walks that road without fear. If you're lying on your deathbed, Betty's your gal. She won't shrink from the changed strange fact of you, from the rasp of your vanishing voice, from your ashy skin, your cracked fingernails, your morphine-addled visions. She will fail to register the blades of your cheekbones, the sweaty mess of your hair. She will see only you, the you beneath. She will place her sweet bird face into the filmy path of your breath and call you honey.

She did this with our mother. With our uncle. With our aunt. And now with Ron, who, despite Betty's tender ministrations, dies anyway.

Afterward we go to Laura's house, where the bed remains, empty and terrifying. "Can I get in it?" Betty asks. My other sisters and I exchange glances. Betty, predictable as the moon, can still muster the power to astonish us. Awestruck, we watch her climb over the metal sides of her surrogate father's bed and lie down where he lay, folding her skeletal hands one over the other. She stares at the ceiling. No one speaks. Eventually, she sits up, gets out, smooths the sheets, says nothing.

We do not ask. Whatever she has done, in our full view, is clearly private. Between her and Ron, perhaps. Or between her and God.

At times like this, I find in Betty's eyes a flame of wisdom, a burning intelligence, a flickering glimpse of a parallel self. She seems older in these moments, not just older than me, but older than everyone, older than her own mortal self. *Divinity* is the word that comes, even to this weak believer; then it's gone, and she's Betty again.

She and Laura share their grief in the only way available to them, to any of us: They keep going.

They resume their After Work Call, and also the six twenty-six, the Weather Report Call.

"What did the weatherman say, Betty Wood?" asks Laura, who has just watched exactly the same report on the same channel.

"Rain."

"Oh, no."

"*Rain*, Laura Ellis."

So it goes, until one day Laura arrives at the shop forgetting things, the first sign of a dementia that often afflicts Down-syndrome souls lucky enough to make it to fifty. For Betty, a familiar rerun commences: appointments, pills, time measured out in "bad" days or "good."

On one of the last good days, the ladies and I take a sunny walk to a wooded path. It's still and fragrant here, the trees looming in silence, but the gals are loud talkers. Birds shy off from branches; unseen creatures flee into the brush. Suddenly Laura remembers her most reliable joke:

"Betty Wood lives in the woods."

I chuckle politely. They howl.

"Betty Wood lives in the woods. Betty Wood lives in the woods. Betty Wood lives in the woods."

After a few minutes of this, even Betty—who will eagerly rewind a steak-knife commercial fifty times—finds it tiresome. They tease each other a lot, these dear friends, but today Laura's "off" button is on the blink.

"Betty Wood lives in the woods."

My own inclination at this point is to find a hollow log in which to install myself until end-time, but instead I slip Betty some sisterly ammunition.

"Guess what?"

They stop. Turn to me in unison. "What?"

"Laura Ellis lives in a trellis."

The ladies find me incandescently hilarious in any case, but *this*—this brilliant riposte—oh, *this* takes the whole cake. They throw back their heads, haw-hawing like horses till they have to stop, take in some wheezing breaths, hang on to their quaking knees.

The rest of the walk—why did I not see this coming?—consists of a mind-numbing call and response:

"Laura Ellis lives in a trellis!"

"Betty Wood lives in the woods!"

In a few weeks' time, Laura Ellis lives not in a trellis but in a hospital bed moved back into the Ellis parlor. Betty is one of the last people Laura still knows. They hold hands. Do the woods-and-trellis joke. Cement the next day's weather forecast. Say goodbye.

Late that night, before Laura slips all the way under, she tells her mother, "Daddy's coming to get me. Can I go?"

"Yes," her mother says. "You can go."

"You won't cry?"

"I'll cry, but it's all right for you to go."

"It's going to be hard on the kids."

Her mother pauses, confused. "What kids?"

"Betty Wood."

She's right. It's hard on Betty Wood. Her grief is deep and old and full of memory. We make a tiny trellis out of sticks to hang on the Christmas tree. Ten times a day, Betty checks to make sure it's still there. We walk through the layering snow, her bony, mittened hand in mine. I say to her quietly, "Betty Wood lives in the woods."

She stops, shakes her bird-fluff head, looks into the unseeable distance, her smile wistful, and there it is again—that glimpse of her what-if life, the brilliant "normal" life she might have lived.

But what of *this* life? What do I think I'm seeing, at these moments, that doesn't already exist? This is Betty:

here, now, her eyes filled with sympathy and understanding. And yes, a kind of brilliance. The intellectual chasm between us divides, and I'm on the wrong side. From here, she looks like the kindly, durable person she has always been: the big sister shoring up against sorrow, charging ahead to the unknown and unknowable, showing her little sister how it's done.

My Sister, Saidee

Susanna Sonnenberg

When my half sister was born I would warm a bottle in the mornings and climb into her crib to give it to her. Our father and her mother slept, and I thought of myself as her protector, an eight-year-old mother, adoring and vigilant. By Saidee's second birthday, our parents had divorced and she was moved away. I felt that my heart had been torn out after all of those weekends of fierce, protective love, of learning her expressions and carrying her from room to room. I was allowed to see her once, staying the night in her mother's home, which smelled of unfamiliar groceries. It wasn't much of a visit, and Saidee, then three, didn't know me. My heart broke all over again.

My father botched his responsibility for his other

daughter, and I didn't see her after that, hearing occasionally of a new stepfather or of a graduation. After I finished college, she visited our father in the city a few times, and we met at his house for awkward exchanges that felt forced, a scripted portrayal of sisterhood. Then, after Saidee married and I was in my early thirties, I took the train to her town. She was late to the depot, and we struggled for conversation on the drive to her house. It was the first time we'd been alone together, and I worried that she wouldn't like me, that I wouldn't like her.

We walked into her living room, and I saw it at once: an antique sofa upholstered in peach silk, the fabric faded by a hundred years of sun. Back home in my living room, where she had never been, sat an antique chair covered in the same silk, faded to this very shade of pale orange, embroidered with these exact flowers in gold and yellow thread. Two women bound by only the thinnest of histories and sharing nothing but an absent father had ended up with the identical obscure, old fabric. Suddenly, I felt the full warmth in the word *sister*, Saidee no longer just someone I knew but flesh and blood, *my* blood. I rounded a hallway corner and was stunned to see a tiny porcelain owl beside her computer. "I keep an owl on my desk," I said, nervous she wouldn't believe me. Over the course of the day, such coincidences kept popping up—the quilted April Cornell pillows in lilac, the same choice of Aveda shampoo—and like people falling in love, we took them as augurs of the relationship to come.

Five years later, Saidee had a daughter. I came for a week to do whatever she needed, walking back into the house that felt and smelled like my own. The baby was always nursing, not yet smiling. One night I walked her around the living room to give Saidee five minutes of a free body before Piper's cries grew strong. Swaying in that perpetual nighttime lilt, I thought, *This must be the feeling grandparents wait for, the summons, the chance to stitch tightly back together the strands that have come loose.* I had walked and rocked Saidee when she was born, loved her, lost her—and tonight, in the summer dark, I held her daughter, the small face a mirror of another little baby and a very young girl.

The Strongest Link

Valerie Monroe

I so loved being pregnant that I wished I could carry my son forever. The bigger I got, the more luxuriously contented I felt. And not just contented: commanding, sorcerous. Who needed to pull *this* bunny out of the hat? In the end, the doctors had to tie me down and remove my son surgically. My obstetrician, who performed the Cesarean section, would say that my cervix had incompletely dilated. That's what *he* thinks. I simply refused to give my baby up.

One evening when my son was about eight months old and I had not yet weaned him, my husband and I left him with a sitter so that we could take in a ballet. By the end of the performance, my throbbing breasts were signaling that I'd been away from the baby long enough. When we walked into our living room the cheerful young sitter was holding him by the hands as he stood, his fat legs wobbly, on her lap. In the moment before he saw me, his expression was one of careful determination, as if he knew he'd had one too many but he could stand on this lap without falling over, dammit, if he just tried hard enough. When his eyes met mine, though, he burst into a brilliant, drooly grin, leaning toward me and bouncing crazily in his excitement. I picked him up. He clutched my neck and started snuffling around in my blouse. As I settled on the couch to nurse him, I felt absolutely whole and complete, the way I'd felt during my pregnancy. It is this powerful, primitive, empathetic connection, this merging, this heady blend of joy, satisfaction, and easy competence that is also the deep grief of motherhood. Because to raise a child successfully, you have to let him go.

As a new parent, I was ambushed by the intensity of the attachment; I had no idea how my feelings would evolve over the course of my son's childhood, from his early loud and stubborn stirrings for independence to his current status as a twenty-year-old college student and world traveler. The first time a sitter took him out in the stroller, I stood at the window, my face pressed to the glass, waiting for her to round the corner on their return. The idea of my son's ever crossing a busy city street alone? You might as well have said that he'd be walking on the moon. Tentatively, I shared a confession with one of my mother friends: "I know I'm not supposed to," I said, "but I love my baby more than I love my husband."

"What can you do?" she said. "Me, too."

Yet day by day, as my son grew, our connection somehow became elastic enough to accommodate his need to establish himself as separate from me: At age three, he suggested a playdate at his best friend Nicolette's house. Really? He wanted me to leave him there alone? "Yep," he said, "pick me up later." At six, he wanted to join an after-school program; at nine, to go to sleep-away camp; at twelve, to spend the weekend at a friend's in the country; at seventeen, to go to school in Minnesota; at nineteen, to study in Japan.

The summer before he left, I couldn't get enough of him; I took every opportunity to be home when he was. One day I asked him if he agreed that the closer a child is to his parents, the farther away he has to go to become independent of them. "I don't know," he said, "maybe." Is that why he chose to go to Japan? "Oh no," he said. Then:

"Maybe." The day he left for Kyoto, I felt as queasy as the first time he'd walked to school alone. Only he was no longer a small, slender shoot bearing the heavy fruit of his backpack, overripe with books—he was tall and strapping, firmly supporting the weight of his decision to leave everything familiar for eight months of the unknown. "We're doing this quickly, like taking off a Band-Aid," he said at the airport when it was time to say goodbye. He hugged my husband and me tightly, turned around, and walked to the plane. I waited till we got to the parking lot and then cried. I cried in short bursts for weeks. I kept thinking, *The sweetest part of my life is over. How can I stand it? What will take its place?*

About halfway through his stay, we visited him. He met us at the airport. He was easy to spot, a couple of heads taller than everyone else in the crowd. "Just follow me," he said, as he led us through the maze of people, passageways, and ticket booths to our train. "Follow me," he said, as he bought our tickets, as he helped us find our room at the hotel. When he was on his own, he rode around Kyoto like the Japanese, on a bicycle. The bike was a little small for him—as was almost everything else—which made him seem bigger than when he'd left home. For two weeks, my husband and I followed our son like baby ducklings. And by the time he put us on the train to Osaka for our flight home, I understood that the sweetest part of my life was not over but that it was expanding, the way the connection between my child and me has always been expanding, to include satisfaction and joy I could never have imagined. I wish I could love everyone in my life the way I love my son: cleanly, without jealousy or neediness, wanting for him happiness, success, strength, and many more people who love him as I do.

The Baby Kaboom

Cristina Nehring

—❖—

Anything can happen in life, especially nothing. These words hung above my desk for years. A quote from French writer Michel Houellebecq, it chilled me with its threat of the eventless existence that lay ahead were I not driven, smart, and daring enough to *make things happen.* By *things* I meant legendary love affairs. Travel. A soaring literary career. Not for me the noisy nursery—my children would be books.

I made strides toward the life I wanted: just enough writerly success to steel my resolve through years of poverty, just enough travel to make me homeless in several countries, just enough love to break my heart. But then I *really* made something happen—and it was not at all what I'd envisioned.

I'd gone to the island of Crete to report a story for a travel magazine and had fallen for a wild-haired boy—ardent, tempestuous, and penniless. Soon I was pregnant, contraceptive pills not withstanding. When I leaped to phone an abortion clinic, he stayed my hand: "I'll do anything for this child," he said. "My family, sister, cousins, nieces will do anything."

I loved him. I thought of friends trying so hard to get pregnant. And I decided the brave thing to do was play the cards I'd been dealt. I asked him to join me for the birth in Paris, where I had a job, health insurance, and a tiny garret I called home.

Eurydice was born during an April hailstorm. Her father was in the delivery room and photographed her first moments. Then he abandoned her. Eurydice had Down syndrome. When she and I returned home after two weeks in the hospital, her father repaired to Crete, changed his number, and told his family never to speak to me again.

Thus ended life as I knew it. Caring for a disabled infant was all consuming. In cafés where I used to write, I now tossed Dice from side to side to calm her colic; when I had to go to the toilet, I perched her on my thighs. Privacy? Romance? Intellectual life? Gone, I believed, for good. People with DS often remain with their parents for life.

But before long my daughter began to laugh. Her first, and for many years her only, vocalization was the sweet, wet smack of a kiss. Rather than make me weaker, she made me stronger. I'd stand over Eurydice's crib as she slept with a smile on her lips, marveling that I was a safe space for this most fragile of creatures. Me: the child woman, full of learned helplessness and debilitating anxiety. I was a protector. The more you do, I soon saw, the more you *can* do. I took Dice on my travel assignments; she came to Morocco and Scotland, Corsica and Tunisia, Sardinia, Greece, and America; she slept in Irish hotel drawers, had diapers changed on baggage trolleys, and spent time with a Mafioso on an island off the coast of Naples. I was prouder of our travels together than I'd ever been of my endlessly easier solo adventures.

By the time Eurydice and I moved our suitcases into an LA isolation room for chemotherapy to treat the acute myeloid leukemia with which she had been diagnosed, we'd packed more life into her two years than others do into fifty. Nonverbal though she was, she'd become my best friend, my accomplice, my heartthrob. I could not imagine her taking any voyage on her own: If death was her next destination, I loved her enough to die with her.

But Eurydice laughed her way through chemo, giving me the greatest lesson in courage I have ever known. Never again will I fear a needle, or blood, or scars. Three ports took their turn in her tiny chest to receive the toxins intended to kill her cancer—which they did. After seven months, when we got out of isolation, we catapulted to an empty lot adjoining the hospital, dug our fingers into bare earth, and exulted in the dirt under our nails. Farewell to the sterility of the hospital room! Mud, dust, dung—welcome!

Life is a series of chapters, and our business is to write them as boldly, as imaginatively, as unapologetically as possible. So many people stare at the same screens, storefronts, and story lines their whole lives. When change—even for the harder—touches us, I say we're lucky.

My life with my daughter has been everything I did not believe I wanted. It slowed my writing career, cut into hundredths my occasions for romance, limited the time I have to waste. But it has provoked insights and wisdom I would never have obtained otherwise, brought into my sphere only the best of men, and multiplied—exponentially—the love I have to live.

A Bigger Love

Anything is possible. Stay open forever,
so open it hurts.

–George Saunders

The Other Woman

Helyn Trickey Bradley

I have a laundry list of reasons for hating the blue recliner: it's lumpy, it's too big for the room, it's covered with scratches from a dog I never knew. It looks like it might've been peed on or accidentally left out in the rain. And it belonged to my husband's dead wife, Karen.

Over and over again, I turn it to face the rest of the room, but because of a slight slope in the floor, the chair stubbornly swivels to face a bookcase that holds a framed photo of Karen sitting in the rumble seat of a Model A with her two young daughters, her blond, chin-length hair shimmering in the sun. I dig up a photo of Gary and me taken after we got engaged, our arms woven tightly, our eyes wide as if we were boarding the biggest ride at the fair.

I place our photo on the bookcase, nudging it next to the picture of Karen and the girls. The frames touch, they are so close. Still, the chair nags at me. I want it gone.

"It's comfortable," Gary argues. "It's functional."

I tell him it looks like it belongs in a fraternity house.

I married Gary, a widower with two young daughters, after a whirlwind romance, the kind with such velocity that it confounds everyone but the two people at its center. We met online, then had dinner on a sticky night in August, when only mosquitoes and lovers linger on park benches. We broke most of the first date rules: He told me of the pain of losing his wife to cancer and the challenges of helping his daughters through their grief. I told him about the toxic decade-long relationship that had left me pessimistic about finding lasting love. By midnight, we'd both admitted that we were open to getting married—him again and me for the first time. It felt like we were spinning through the universe, two shooting stars shivering with speed. The following month, Gary introduced me to his daughters: Tonya, twelve, energetic and twinkly eyed, and Lizzie, a five-year-old with a honey-colored bob and a jack-o'-lantern smile. Three months later, we were engaged. Less than a year after our first date, I became, at forty-one, a first-time wife and mother of two. In so many ways it was a dream come true, and I wanted badly to believe that moving into the home Gary had shared with Karen would be as seamless and wonderful as falling in love with her husband had been. Loving Gary was easy. Loving Gary's daughters was easy. Loving Karen was not.

The house was saturated with her. When we made peppermint tea, we used Karen's kettle. When we baked pumpkin muffins, we used Karen's oven mitts. Mail addressed to her still came to the house. I'd hoped I would grow to treasure Karen's primary-colored Fiesta dishes, her wedding dress, pressed and hanging at the back of our closet, waiting for Tonya or Lizzie. Instead, I wondered what kind of woman would buy a gingham shower curtain and leave the walls in her home a numbing shade of Landlord White. I resented the recipe notes, penned in her no-frills handwriting, that dropped out of her vegetarian cookbooks. In my heart, I knew that it was irrational to envy a dead person, someone who would never watch her daughters sing solos in school plays or wave goodbye to them as they shuffled nervously out the front door on first dates. But I couldn't help it: I wanted to claw the ruffled valances she'd hung in the kitchen. I even started drinking my morning coffee without cream to delay confronting the photo of Karen and Tonya taped to the refrigerator.

Gary and I had dismissed the idea of selling the house; the economy was sagging, and real estate was not fetching the prices it once had. More important, we didn't want to move the girls from the only home they'd known so soon after losing their mother. And anyway, I liked the white cottage with the picket fence, snuggled in amid towering Douglas firs on a street where neighbors waved. I was sure that with a little paint and some new furniture, the house Karen and Gary had renovated could become my home, too.

So we painted. We bought a lovely sofa set and changed the shower curtains. We tore out the wood-burning stove in the living room in favor of a gas fireplace. I arranged my John Updike novels and volumes of Mary Oliver's poetry on the bookshelves. But the blue chair remained— and so, it seemed, did Karen's hold on my house.

I was jealous that Karen had loved my husband for seventeen years. She'd known him as a young man, when starting his own woodworking business was just a dream he whispered about under the covers. Karen had loved my husband before children—when, I imagined, sleeping late, romantic weekends at the coast, and long, uninterrupted conversations were routine. I hated learning that Gary had proposed to Karen on a cliff overlooking the Pacific Ocean. Pausing to study their wedding photo in a corner of Gary's home office, I spied a young couple squinting and ecstatic in the sun outside the Chapel of Love in Las Vegas, grinning like they'd just pulled off a bank heist.

I've had girlfriends, most of them sane and successful, who've made voodoo dolls out of their lovers' ex-wives or past girlfriends. I can't do that to Karen: It's distasteful to speak ill of the dead, much less stick effigies of them with pins. I can't even complain about her to my friends without feeling like a heel.

To commemorate Karen's death each April, Gary and the girls release balloons with messages they've written on paper hearts attached to the strings. On the second anniversary of her death, Gary and I had been engaged for four months. I knew I was officially part of the family when Tonya and Lizzie selected a red balloon for me to release, too. But I had trouble writing a message. I wasn't sure what Karen would want to hear from me, the woman who'd sneaked into her house, slept with her husband, and presumed to know how to mother her two babies. I sat with a pencil poised over my blank paper heart. Finally I just scribbled "Thank you" and quickly folded the paper twice so no one could glimpse what I'd written. It felt like such a silly, weak message, but what could I say? The truth and incredible irony is that Gary, Tonya, and Lizzie's loss was my gain.

One summer, while Gary, the girls, and I were on the Oregon coast, we stopped at a favorite local restaurant following an afternoon spent building sand castles and splashing in the frigid Pacific. As we waited for our cheeseburgers and fries, I leaned over and brushed some sand from Tonya's eyebrows. Someone at the table, maybe Lizzie, began to hum, and soon the whole family was singing "She'll Be Coming 'Round the Mountain" and laughing about how none of us except Gary could remember the lyrics. We were still singing when Tonya looked at me and stopped short, her face stricken. She turned her gaze to the ocean tumbling outside the window, but the tears at the edges of her eyes told me what had happened: She'd lost herself in time and had turned toward me expecting to see Karen.

We hadn't been together a year when Gary and I discovered I was pregnant. During my second trimester, we learned that our baby was too small, and the doctor advised bed rest. Heavy and uncomfortable, I spent my days sipping protein shakes and drifting in and out of fitful naps. Gary and the girls would gather in the bedroom each afternoon and tell me their news. It occurred to me that they must have done the same during Karen's final months. As her body withered in hospice care, Karen's adjustable home hospital bed had been placed along the west wall to give her a view of the busy dining room. My queen-size sleigh bed now sat in the same place—but while I was lying under the covers waiting for a new life to take hold, Karen had been waiting for her own to end.

Twisting in a tangle of sheets, I thought about how Karen, too, must have looked out the window to watch the neighbors trudge through the drizzle with golden retrievers tugging on their leashes. Surely she also saw the school bus motor down our quiet street every afternoon, filled with boisterous children. Maybe she lifted her head and smiled when she heard the thumping of small feet, Tonya's earnest attempts to channel Adele, and Lizzie's lament of "I'm hungry!"

I began to grill Gary for details about this woman whose life I'd come to inhabit. From him I learned that Karen had planted King Edward daffodil bulbs each fall, that she made her own granola, that she could watch any movie starring Cary Grant ten times without tiring. Gary told me how on a blustery Friday afternoon in February 2009, Karen had gathered her daughters close on her bed and, with Gary's help, explained that the bad cells were beating the good cells, and that she was going to die. Lying there in the room we shared, I couldn't imagine how she'd summoned the courage.

Every so often during those months of bed rest, when Gary and the girls were out, I'd wander through the quiet house, letting my fingertips drift along the same countertops that Karen's hands had touched. I'd sit at the dining room table, clutching a mug of ginger tea and a box of saltines, fighting off morning sickness. And I'd wonder whether Karen, who had miscarried twice before she and Gary adopted Tonya and Lizzie, had sat at this same table feeling sick to her stomach. I was certain she'd experienced the anxiety that was now consuming me, the heavy possibility of so much loss. In life, we have little control over whom we fall in love with and when; which babies flourish in our bellies and which don't; when we die and whom we leave behind, bobbing and gulping in our wake.

In January 2012, I delivered a healthy baby girl, and Gary and I became swamped with around-the-clock feedings, diaper changes, and swaddling and re-swaddling our squirmy infant. I was so overwhelmed by new motherhood that I nearly forgot my jealousy of Karen—until one afternoon when I sank deep into her old blue chair to feed my daughter. Holding my warm baby, I lifted my foot and the recliner swiveled to face the bookcase. From there, I could see an array of photos: Gary and me at our wedding; Tonya and Lizzie goofing around at the beach; our newborn, her hair wet from the bath, her eyes starry with wonder. I felt a sudden surge of gratitude for my oddly constructed family—including Karen, who will always be here: in photos, in memories joyous and heartbreaking, in her careful recipe notes, and in her blue chair, which still isn't pretty, but is starting to feel like home.

It Only Has to Make Sense to You

Aimee Swartz

I met Jackie shortly after I left a relationship that made my world feel small and crushing—that made romance feel impossible. Which was fine, since Jackie was only a friend; she'd never even dated a woman. She was disarming, generous, a world-class doler-outer of advice. She played me her favorite albums—the Rolling Stones' *Beggars Banquet*, Quasi's *Featuring "Birds"*—and sang every word. She told me stories about her girlhood in a hippie cult, about riding a dirt bike through California's Central Valley. She was so *cool*—uninhibited and completely herself. Her air of calm made her easy to be around and, as time passed, hard to be away from. She made me feel like everything was going to be okay.

Which was ironic.

Jackie was thirty-five when she was diagnosed with multiple myeloma, an incurable blood cancer that typically afflicts people twice her age. The doctors told her that most patients were lucky to live five years. By the time I saw Jackie in a documentary about cancer and reached out to ask her where I could buy the hat she wore in the film (FUCK CANCER, it read), she had held on for seven years. The treatments she was getting would prolong her life but could not save it.

This fact had shaved a layer off Jackie's social graces: She had ditched the polite filters of conversation and gave others a thrilling pass to do the same. One of the first things she said to me was, "What's your story?" She wanted to know everything about me, even if it meant asking prying questions. And so we became very close very fast. Our talks meandered through the peaks and valleys of our lives, our uncensored histories. Sometimes, if it got too late, I'd stay over at her place, where the possibility of touching hands or bumping elbows in the night kept me awake. (She had a couch, but in typical Jackie fashion was letting someone crash on it—so we shared her bed.) That I was nursing any romantic hope sneaked up on me; it was weeks before I noticed that when we hugged goodbye and Jackie pressed her face into my neck, my knees went wobbly.

But I still didn't see her as a romantic prospect. She had taken herself off the market.

"No one wants to be with someone on her way out," Jackie said one night. The reality of her cancer—meds that made her drifty, the sudden limitations on her aspirations, the imminent full stop—had been too much for some of Jackie's friends, who showed up less and less and then disappeared altogether. She no longer believed that anyone would stay when things got heavy.

Maybe it was the way her eyes locked onto mine as she said these words, or the uncertainty in her voice, as though she were hoping I would disagree. Whatever it was, the moment she told me no one would love her again, I knew I did.

I spent the summer in a state of cautious euphoria. Jackie didn't look sick, and we were having fun, so I put fear out of my mind. Call it denial; my friends called it a wanton courting of heartbreak. They peppered me with questions I couldn't answer: Was I ready to be a caregiver? What would happen after she was gone? I kept to my drumbeat—*I feel something real; I think she feels it, too.* But when I let myself think about falling for someone with a terminal illness, the rosy vision I had for my future faded to gray.

It would be weeks more before Jackie and I finally kissed one balmy night. It felt as if it had always been a feature of our friendship, as natural as breathing. Still, she, too, was concerned for me. "It's not fair for you to have to deal with this," Jackie said that night. Then she fell asleep. I listened to her breath, feeling the weight of my love. It was bigger than cancer, bigger than fear. I would lose her someday. But I couldn't let it be *that* day, not when there could still be so many left.

We've been together for more than three years. There are good times, and there are times when Jackie is so weak, she can't put on her shoes. How will it feel to watch her slip away? I think about her dying in our house and my living there alone. I still don't know the answers to my friends' questions. I don't know what will happen, or when. All I know is that I want to be with Jackie, in heartache and joy, sickness and health, for however long we get.

The Cupped Hands

Pam Houston

—❖—

Two years ago, I was lying on a table with needles sticking into my ears, neck, belly, ankles, and between my toes, when my acupuncturist said to me, out of nowhere, "Well, you know, Pam, you are protected."

Denise was treating me for debilitating lower-back pain, after the MRI had said "severely degenerated L4/5 disk," and the family doctor had said "eventual wheelchair," and the specialist had said "Call me when you become incontinent," and the surgeon had said "Sure, we can operate, but it probably won't work."

Acupuncture had worked, steadily, deeply, undeniably, and eliminating pain was only the beginning; with each treatment I was becoming calmer, more solidly grounded in the center of my life. Denise is a wonder: smart, hilarious, ultra-intuitive, massively tuned in. When she said I was protected, I knew she was talking about something bigger than job security or health insurance.

"I do know," I said, because somehow, unaccountably, I did. Denise patted my arm and I closed my eyes, and that is the first time I saw the cupped hands.

Before I go on, let me say that I was born and raised in Trenton, New Jersey. I am an obsessive-compulsive checkbook balancer, I love football and ice hockey, and I got a perfect score on the analytical portion of the Graduate Record Exam. So when serendipitous—even uncanny—encounters occur in my life, I have to squint at them from all angles before I am willing to believe.

There was the time, years ago, when I had missed my plane at LAX Airport and Carlos Castaneda walked up (as if he knew me, though of course he did not), introduced himself, and gave me four essential pieces of advice about my life. There was the time I was sitting in Granzella's, a roadside attraction off the I-5 south of Redding, in California's grim Central Valley, drinking bad coffee, telling a twenty-year-old story about William Hurt (whom I didn't know either, but who had once changed my life by the way he read a story onstage), only to look up from my coffee to see that Hurt—all dressed in white like some angel of the interstate—had just walked through the front door.

The cupped hands, though, were on a different plane of uncanny than the sudden appearance of a Yaqui mystic or the ability to conjure an Academy Award–winning actor by saying his name. These hands were not actual, not in the flesh, as William's and Carlos's had been when I shook them. I saw these hands only in my mind's eye, and yet they were as insistent, as undeniable as anything I have seen or felt in my life. The cupped hands were grown-up hands—lined, fleshy, and weathered, poised to receive possibly water, possibly something water only stands for. They were there, I was given to understand, to catch me if I fell.

A few days later I was walking with my dog in the alfalfa fields outside Davis, California, noticing that in spite of some disappointments I was coping with (a painful but inevitable breakup, severe budget cuts at work), I was feeling happy, almost exhilarated. I recalled the inverse of that moment, times when everything in my life had been going great and I felt unaccountably sad. The possibility of untethering happiness and sadness from circumstance felt frightening and wonderful, like a new brand of freedom.

The sun was setting in the Central Valley haze, leaving a kind of pink mouth against a white sky, and somehow in and through that rose-colored opening, I saw/felt those cupped hands again. What had begun as exhilaration became a quiet, permeating ecstasy that hung around long enough for me to find myself humming, then laughing. I fought the urge to turn cartwheels all the way back to my truck.

A few months later I was sitting on the opposite side of the continent, far out on the long rocky breakwater in Provincetown Harbor, Massachusetts, under a similarly pink-slashed sunset, talking to the sea and the sky. Some people would call this praying, and I might one day, too, so I began, as I believe all prayers should, with gratitude. *Thank you for the sunset, thank you for my friends, thank you for the pain that is gone from my back. Thank you, that is, both for the wake-up call of pain, and for its subsequent relief.*

I watched the tide rush out under the giant slabs of granite beneath me.

"Okay," I said, out loud this time, which felt both ridiculous and better. "I think I am finally ready for you to send me a big, deep, generous love." I'll admit I didn't know whom I was praying to. Something that might be called Ocean and might be called God, and that manifested itself to me occasionally as cupped hands.

"But if you don't think I am ready for big love," I continued, "then maybe just a little romance to keep the conversation going." A great blue heron landed in the reeds nearby. "And if I'm not even ready for that, maybe just a sign that I'm on the right path."

Satisfied with my prayer, I trained my eyes on the heron. A dapper little man was approaching on the jetty, wearing short shorts in psychedelic colors and a yellow shirt, walking a Westie, which was wearing a sweater even though the day was quite warm. The man said, "Lovely place to sit and think, isn't it?"

"Yes," I said, "it surely is."

He never broke stride, but he grinned as he passed. "You are a good person," he said. "It's all going to be okay."

I watched him recede along the horizon, the tops of the big rocks turning green and gold and purple in the encroaching twilight. "Thanks," I told the thing that is part God and part Ocean. "That was just what I had in mind."

It was exactly two weeks later when I found myself in Taos, New Mexico, talking with a poet named Greg Glazner, someone I had not known until chance put us on a shared bill at a night full of literary readings. We were in his hotel room—not as salacious as it sounds, but the conversation was having that delicious accelerated quality that can happen sometimes with strangers, and before long I was telling him about Denise, and the alfalfa fields, and the cupped hands.

"These hands?" he asked, holding his hands just like the ones in my mind's eye, with a look of such intensity on his face that it scared me.

"Well, you know," I said, backpedaling, "cupped hands as metaphor." What had made me want to share my fledgling spiritual realizations with a complete stranger, anyway? "Some kind of safety or support."

"Oh," he said, "I know those hands," and he reached into his briefcase and pulled out a greeting card with a photo of hands on the front, fleshy, weathered, cupped, and catching a stream of cold, clear water. "Look," he said, and held the card out to me. "And look," he said, pointing to the yard-sale-quality print over the standard-issue hotel bed. There were the soft lines of a woman's face, below it only the suggestion of a body, and below it, in sharper detail than anything else, her open, waiting hands.

The rest, as they say, is history. Greg and I have been together going on two years now, and though no relationship is made without effort, this one is proving to be that big love I prayed for on the Provincetown rocks. I don't know why, and I don't know why now, but I do know I would have to be some kind of arrogant to squint too hard at my good fortune this time. Denise says it is simple: I had to learn how to ask for help before I could receive it. Now when life gets hard and I start to lose faith, I put myself back in that alfalfa field, where a smudged sky opened up and invited me inside it, momentarily illuminating my connection to everything larger than me.

Heart-Prints

Oprah Winfrey

—✦—

What I know about love I mostly learned on TV. In twenty-five years of hosting my show, I saw what love can do in the most ordinary moments (watching a mother take her child to the first day of school) and the most extraordinary (strangers offering their homes to strangers in the aftermath of Hurricane Katrina). Whenever you've been touched by love, a heart-print lingers, so that you're always reminded of the feeling of being cared for, knowing that, to someone, you mattered.

I remember leaving the Houston Astrodome early in the morning eight days after Katrina hit. Most people were still sleeping as we finished taping our show. A young father in a clean white T-shirt was carrying his sleeping six-year-old daughter over his shoulder, and I stopped to ask, "How you making out, sir?"

He replied, "I'm gonna make it, 'cause I've already survived Katrina and now I'm just moving on love—and I ain't never felt so much love in my whole life."

"Wow," I said. "You are gonna make it."

Lots of guests over the years left heart-prints on me. Mattie Stepanek, a child poet whose only goal was to spread peace, was one of the wisest people I've ever met. If angels come to earth, he was definitely one of them. He came to remind us of who we are: love incarnate. When he died at age thirteen, I made a book of all the e-mails we had exchanged. He was love to me.

Erin Kramp was an "ordinary" mother. She discovered she had breast cancer, and while she was fighting to live, she prepared her six-year-old daughter, Peyton, for life the best way she knew how. She started recording tapes, more than 100 total, about everything she could think of to tell her daughter as she grew up, knowing there wouldn't be enough time to say it all: how to put on makeup, get boys to like you, choose friends, and dress well; stories about herself; her favorite songs, foods, and movies. Her most awesome gift, I thought, was this message: "If God decides to take me to heaven, I'm going to be looking for another soul to bring to Daddy. So I want you to know that I would very much bless Daddy remarrying."

Four years later, when Peyton's father wanted to remarry, he went to his daughter first. The ten-year-old said she needed more time to get to know her father's bride-to-be, so he waited. When Peyton said she was ready, Doug proposed. That same night, Peyton wrote a letter welcoming her new mom. Awesome! The love exchanged among Erin, Peyton, Doug, and his new wife, Cheryl, was so authentic it made us all rejoice when we witnessed it on the show. That's what love does: It fills you up, mends the tattered and broken spaces in your spirit. It makes you feel whole. Not everybody has an Erin Kramp in her life, but love is all around and ever available. I know this for sure.

Sometimes in the thick of life, when my to-do list is longer than the day and people are lined up waiting for meeting after meeting, I just stop and still myself. And look at a tree. A flower. The sun's light reflecting off the window. And I remember that love is available. I inhale it, exhale, and get back to work.

I recently reread an e-mail from Mattie, dated November 22, 2001. He was eleven at the time. He'd recently seen *The Color Purple* (the movie), and he wrote, "This year my mom and I are both wearing purple for Thanksgiving. I'm thankful for things like safety during terrorism, for food and material things like that, and for the people in the circle of my life, like my mom and Sandy, the Moxes upstairs, and you. For things that God has given us, just because we are loved. Purple. Gentle breezes. Crickets. Shooting stars. Laughter. Feathers. I'm thankful that things *are*, so while *we* are, we can have gifts every day if we just open our hearts and spirits to them."

Words of wisdom from an eleven-year-old.

Look around, feel the love.

Contributors

Martha Beck is a life coach whose most recent book, *The Martha Beck Collection: Essays for Creating Your Right Life, Volume One*, is an anthology of her work in *O, The Oprah Magazine*, where she's been a columnist since 2001. Her other books include *Leaving the Saints, Finding Your Own North Star, The Joy Diet, Steering by Starlight*, and *Finding Your Way in a Wild New World*.

Helyn Trickey Bradley has been a contributor to CNN, PBS, and *The Oregonian*. She lives in Portland, Oregon, with her husband and three daughters, and is at work on a memoir.

Andrea King Collier is a journalist and author whose books include *Still with Me: A Daughter's Journey of Love and Loss* and *The Black Woman's Guide to Black Men's Health*.

Andrew Corsello, a correspondent for *GQ*, lives in San Francisco with his wife and two sons.

Amy Dickinson writes the "Ask Amy" advice column, which is syndicated throughout North America, and is a regular on NPR's *Wait Wait . . . Don't Tell Me!* Her memoir, *The Mighty Queens of Freeville*, was a *New York Times* bestseller. She's at work on a sequel.

Allison Glock is a longtime journalist and coauthor of the young adult series Changers and the memoir *Beauty Before Comfort.*

Alice Bingham Gorman, a writer of fiction and nonfiction, splits her time between the west coast of Florida and Maine.

Pam Houston directs the literary nonprofit Writing by

Writers and teaches writing around the world. She is the author of five books, including *Cowboys Are My Weakness* and *Contents May Have Shifted*.

Elizabeth Kelsey is an essayist whose articles on friendship, love, and travel have appeared in numerous national magazines. She is currently writing a memoir about her cross-cultural marriage.

Walter Kirn's most recent book is *Blood Will Out*, a memoir of his friendship with the con man and convicted murderer Clark Rockefeller. His work has appeared in the *New Yorker*, the *New York Times*, and the *New Republic*. His novels *Up in the Air* and *Thumbsucker* have been made into feature films.

Lisa Kogan, *O, The Oprah Magazine*'s writer at large and advice columnist ("Dear Lisa") is the author of the essay collection *Someone Will Be with You Shortly*.

Cathleen Medwick is literary editor of *More* magazine and the author of *Teresa of Avila: The Progress of a Soul*.

Valerie Monroe, beauty director for *O, The Oprah Magazine*, is author of the memoir *In the Weather of the Heart*.

Cristina Nehring, PhD., has written several books, including *A Vindication of Love* and *Journey to the Edge of the Light*. Her essays have appeared in numerous publications, including the *Atlantic, Harper's,* and *Condé Nast Traveler*. She lives in Paris with her daughter.

Susanna Sonnenberg is author of *Her Last Death* and *She Matters: A Life in Friendships*. She lives in Missoula, Montana.

Elizabeth Strout won the Pulitzer Prize for her novel *Olive Kitteridge*, which was made into an HBO special starring Frances McDormand. Her new novel, *My Name Is Lucy Barton*, is slated for 2016.

Aimee Swartz is a freelance health writer based in Atlanta and Washington, D.C. She's written for the *Washington Post* and the *Atlantic*.

Abigail Thomas's most recent book is the memoir *What Comes Next and How to Like It.*

Ellen Tien is a former staff writer for the *New York Times.* She lives in Manhattan with her husband and son.

Patricia Volk is a Guggenheim recipient and the author of two novels, two collections of stories, and two volumes of essays. She lives in New York City.

Monica Wood wrote the bestselling novel *Any Bitter Thing* and is author of the forthcoming *The One-in-a-Million Boy.*

extracts reading groups
competitions books new
discounts extracts
competitions extracts
books new
events books
extracts new titles reading groups
interviews
events extracts
discounts
new books events
events new
discounts extracts discounts
www.panmacmillan.com
extracts events reading groups
competitions books extracts new